Visualization, The Prophet Sees In Adullam

Ken Cox

REJOICE
Essential Publishing

Ken Cox/Rejoice Essential Publishing
PO BOX 512
Effingham, SC 29541
www.republishing.org

Unless otherwise indicated, scripture is taken from the King
James Version.

Visualization, The Prophet Sees In Adullam/Ken Cox

ISBN-13: 9781956775594
LCCN: 2023904388

Table Of Contents

Introduction

The experience of experiencing people never grows old. The prophetic ensures us we will share that. There's an experience to be had as to how you respond to people when everything you're living is the opposite of who you are or who you feel. This will hit home when God has told you something, and your life is the opposite.

Hello, my friend, and welcome to *Visualization, The Prophet Sees In Adullam*. We will look at ourselves as we explore the very essence of seeing and how difficult the process is when a word is given, and the reality of that word has not manifested. This is real-world stuff.

Welcome to David's world. His life is central, as we demonstrate, and visualize finding yourself in an odd place in life. We will explore David's prophetic gift and see how it relates to your gift and life at this very moment. *Visualization, The Prophet Sees In Adullam* will be told by David's life and other prophetic peers. They will give us much to relate to.

Answer this question, what's more difficult? Living a life with all eyes on you, or the fact that you know you don't align with the standards of that same life that you have claimed. Some people will constantly remind you of that fact. What do you do? Your life is tied to drama, and you are supposed to be the prophet.

David, in my humble opinion, is a prophet of epic proportions. This work will reflect significantly on his development and the example it provides for our development as prophets. Seers of this generation seek the David experience; it will benefit us. We can almost always find ourselves in some difficult situation. We are called to that, but let's, be advised of the work we must do on ourselves.

This is what we see in the life of David. Stay connected to the issue of finding yourself in difficult times. The opportunity that God has given me to work with prophets and seers has shown me that this is an essential work within us we must accomplish. The experience is priceless.

Notice that there are similar issues with prophets of all different prophetic mantles and, most of all, cultures. This is prophetic training and the prophetic process of development. The more you study it, the more you will understand it. Visualization births revelation and the needed mentality to function at high levels in the prophetic.

Before ascending to the Body of Christ, we must understand ourselves to be God's chosen servant. We need some training. This book is about a specialized type of prophetic training called *Visualization, The Prophet Sees In Adullam*. Let's see if it fits your mantle.

CHAPTER 1

Adullam, The Prophet's Essential Process

The question that every prophet will face is, what do you do when your life does not look like who you are? Have you ever been there? Have you ever considered that you can see your promise and chaos occupying the same space in your life, all simultaneously? Did you ever wonder if others saw it? You are anointed, but it does not look or seem that way.

Have you ever told someone not to worry, and yet you did? You worried behind the scenes. You were off to yourself, and what you spoke, what you stood for, you contradicted it with your actions and life.

Prophet, the prophecy was from God, and it was on point, but the situation as you monitor it seems more and more chaotic. This is why you need to clearly understand the process of Adullam in a prophet's life.

1 Samuel 22, we see the life of David in the cave of Adullam. Here we have David, a leader, warrior, and for me, a prophet. A prophet whom God has spoken of has his heart. David is not perfect, but he is a human, and yes, he has his faults.

Some say David is not a prophet, while others see him as a particular type of prophet. David is also one whose life mimics the prophetic journey of developing a serviceable prophet of God. That will be hard to doubt, as you will see throughout this book.

Prophet, as we look at David's life lets, look at your life and see what God is doing. David is a king and a leader, but his life does not reflect who he is. Prophet, how do you handle that? Rest assured, you will be faced with it. Prophet, has your life looked one way, and your promise looked another?

Let's focus on David, who has escaped Gath, a Philistine city, and now he escapes to The Cave of Adullam. Those whom David once led are now hunting him. David is safer with his enemies than with those he was once leading. Every now-generation prophet has someone they do not feel good around. We are human.

Every now generation seer has had someone turn on them, and if they do not, keep living, and you will experience this as David did.

Some of our haters may be family whom you are reluctant to claim. They always greet you with a word of conflict or criticism. They always say a comment that takes away from you or finds fault in you somehow. They seem never to fail, and it's almost like they rehearsed it.

Most of us, who have experienced this, have heard it and dealt with it in some manner. Sometimes we feel better with people we don't know very well. This could be people you meet at a meeting or people who may not understand the prophetic. Imagine that you feel better and more accepted around the ones who know of you rather than the ones who know you. Allow me to welcome you to the prophetic community. Can you see this in David's life? Compare his brothers and Saul versus those grateful that he defeated Goliath.

Can you relate to David? Think about this prophet. You have done for them; they rejected you. You have prayed for them, and they still rejected you. They clearly have not appreciated you, and they have barely tolerated you.

Like David, you run to Gath and attempt to dwell among the Philistines, and now you escape to Adullam as a last resort.

Remember, I am asking you to look at David as a leader and a prophet who will become king.

Let's examine this: we see David being discovered in Gath, and he plays crazy to get out of it. David has been pushed to his limit even the King of Gath has called him crazy. Life has taught me that if God uses you, expect at some point in your life to be pushed to your limit by life itself.

This will be your proof and test of God, all in the same scenario. God is a master at directing our lives with opposites and allowing us to see, understand and seek Him for our refuge. The private prophetic development continues for David as he seeks refuge in Adullam.

1st Samuel 22 shows us precisely that. David has sought refuge, now in Adullam. Look at this, David is currently a king, a leader, and a prophet in a crisis. Do you know what it may feel like to be a prophet in crisis? I have already mentioned that everything is going wrong, and despite what God spoke through Samuel, it looks different. Prophet, can you relate to this?

Who can relate? You're a prophet in a crisis. Things have happened in your life, and you're almost ready to quit.

People have left you, betrayed you, you have seen them on social media throwing off on you, and now you ask, how can I be a prophet without a known prophetic mantle? This is where you start to develop that oh-so-personal relationship with God needed for the prophetic.

Things have gone bad for you in your mind, and you have lost creditability with your peers and now look at you. This is where you are at; think about it.

What do you do? Now you do, you say to yourself, "What is the solution that you must realize and follow and accept?" So many prophets get to this point in their life and stop. They get here and quit.

David could have quit, but he did not. David could have run, but he did not. Prophet, accept this because it is so critically important; as you will see in chapter *1 Samuel chapter 2:30*, I will expand on this point by talking about Prophetic Honor in Chapter Four of this book.

What is the answer? Is it easy but not so simple when going through a storm? The answer comes when you realize that success with man differs from success with God. This, for a prophet, can be a painful lesson, and even more painful when God sends a mentor into your life, and you reject them because you are so caught up proving to everyone that God has directed you to do great work.

How often have we seen anointed people labor in small places that seem to reflect disrespect and abandonment from close comrades, and yet just a faithful few continue? Those of you in dry lands can and should relate to this.

Many of today's now-generation prophets, with a global anointing, labor in secluded lands. David shows us the example of allowing God to dictate success in our lives. Somebody say, "Right now, order my steps, Lord, I will trust you!"

Prophets look at David; his situation looks like he is a useless, washed-up leader. His situation made him appear crazy and useless; no one wanted to be around him. David has now run to the Cave of Adullam. It looks one way, but he is still a leader. You are going through this right now, but you are still a leader and a prophet despite what is going on in your life.

David is a king, yet he is in a cave, but he is still a king. The situation looks bleak, like it is ruined, yet David runs to Adullam. Adullam represents a place of refuge for David. Every prophet needs to have a place of Adullam.

This is where finding ourselves we find the prophet within us, just as David found himself. Let me caution you as a reader. Please read my book *"Meeting The Prophet in My Reflection."* This will help some of you understand who you are in the prophetic as you look to identify your mantle. The issue is to find yourself.

The prophetic gift's diversity will help you be faithful to God and yourself. Why? You may ask. The reason is that when you find yourself, you will find that you are the only one like you. This will scare and frighten some. You will never find yourself until you are prepared to handle the fact that there is only one you.

How many of us need a place of refuge in our lives? A place where we find ourselves because we have run from a place of confusion, disappointment, and disrespect in our lives. The place in our life where we finally realize that we are who we are and it does not matter how anyone may or may not feel about us.

Some of us have run from people we know, others have run from our peers who did not understand us, and here we are. Can we see ourselves in a place where we function as a refuge in a place that provides for us to gather ourselves? We are in the cave of Adullam just as David was, and we are also.

Here you are a prophet, and no one to prophesy to, no one to speak to or pour into. The fact is that if you are really a prophet of God, then being in your personal Cave of Adullam does not change who you are. This is a fact that we often overlook. Think of it, just because a medical doctor is sick does not take away from the fact that they are a doctor.

Prophet, just because they rejected you in the family, church, and community, did not change the fact that God has called you to be a prophet. That is a fact that you must accept and realize. Build the mentality to realize this fact. This is a critical fact.

Now generation prophets listen; the prophetic education is so based and built on experience that joins us in walks with the formal education of the prophetic gift called prophetic training. So many of us forget that fact.

We must realize today that we can be anointed to be a prophet, a seer, and yet we have not been able to acquire the experience needed to fulfill the call. This is a fact that can't be disputed while we may differ on what prophetic education is, experience is an undisputed teacher.

Today in our now generation, we must realize that we can be anointed and need the deposited experience to function on the assigned level of God. This is what happens to so many of us in the prophetic ministry.

We are looking for public acknowledgment without the benefit of a deposited experience. Have you ever noticed that God will send you a deposited experience through a mentor, yet we reject the mentor and forfeit the deposited experience? How many of us have had to learn this the hard way?

We may be anointed, yet we are not ready to function in the way God wants us to. We need to benefit from the deposited experiences of our lives. David was so excellent at that. Look at yourself.

Can you relate? Like David, you had to process the information quickly and act, even when it was not in your favor. Experience is needed to function in our lives as a temperature of how we, as prophets, are to be balanced in our lives for God's purposes.

We should be able to operate in any situation, whether we have a lack or plenty. David operated without the support of those he started with. This is something that happens in the lives of prophets.

This is the essence of a deposited experience. There is no substitute for this. Our journeys are different yet relevant in their familiarity with prophetic development.

I want you to think about this and realize that not everyone around you will cater to or support you. We, you, and I may not get the support. The fact is, it will not take away from the fact that you are who you are.

Like David, so many of you have a powerful anointing. You will learn that a powerful anointing requires going through a series of painful apprenticeships. This is a fact and a hard lesson to realize, that it could be happening to you.

This is because God will not give you such an awesome anointing and not balance it with pain. Prophets, seers, watchman, and even apostles understand that your pain is directly related to your anointing.

Welcome to the essence of what prophetic development is all about. This is how we develop as prophets. The haters of the prophet make us who we are! They help us respect and appreciate what God has given us. We know who we are as we see who hates or rejects us. We are the Seers of God, which does not make us popular.

More often than now, you will be hated. Prophet, like David, you are hated because of who you are. David is a king, hated by a king. Imagine that you can be a prophet hated by your peers.

Prophet, understand who you are and how those around you feel about you. Learn how to thank God for real covenant relationships. God provides them in your life for a reason.

We are all subject to the reality of new levels that bring us new challenges, and especially new devils. We are just like David; a new level has brought him to a level he is not familiar with. We welcome you again to prophetic growth and development.

Now again, would you imagine David in Adullam? Prophet, also imagine yourself, and yet some of you are there right now. David has great faith, but he also has fear. The question is not that David has faith, but he has an equal measure of fear, which is why he ran. Prophet, if you're going to grow, if you're going to develop, then you must be honest with yourself.

David, God's man of power, God's man of faith, has run, he has played crazy, and he has now retreated to the cave of Adullam. We see a great believer, but he has unbelief also. Can David demonstrate visualization and see himself?

Let's not fool ourselves, like David; we have both belief and unbelief living in us simultaneously. He is looking to find out what he needs to do next.

David has survived and needs to know what to do next. Prophets, how many of us have been there, we escaped the drama, and now we are safe, and yet we are still unfinished. Again prophets, we must look at the state that I am in.

The state I am in does not define who I am in God. David has made it to a place of relevance to deal with his shortcomings. He is in Adullam, and he can look at himself now.

Like a prophet, he is asking himself what is next after being betrayed, put down, rejected, and forced to face a hidden weakness; now he has run, is somewhat stable in this cave, and asks what is next. Prophet, have you ever been there, or maybe now you are there, and you ask yourself what is next?

Prophets, can you understand being in this place in your life? David is in a layover state in Adullam. God has put you in Adullam, and David is there, and you as a prophet are there, and the reason is you now have finally found out who you are without any of "them" in your life. This is a place of self-discovery. You now discover who you are without any of their help or any of their dreams in your life.

This is the place of your self-worth, you regain your courage, and you realize that God is for you. The reality is that if no one is for you, here is where you realize that God is for you. Every prophet must recognize this and adopt this.

To those prophets who have uncommon gifts in your life, you now start to realize why things happened and what they happened for. You now know and understand how to listen and how to trust.

Every prophet needs to realize that Adullam is where you discover yourself and realize that God moves in His own ways and not to your or anyone else's satisfaction. God does it His way and not your way. You want victory, and God gives you understanding. This is what Adullam is all about.

Prophet like David, you will go and escape to your personal Adullam when you realize that the ones who know you will follow and seek you out. David's family came and sought him out as his family saw him differently.

This is something that every prophet needs to understand, God says to stand still, and God will allow some of your old associations to come back into your life when you grow past the bitterness of how you were treated.

God puts your life together so you can handle the hurt of your past. This is why the family will do an about-face on you because, in the cave of Adullam, God transforms us as He did in David's life. The process is worth the product it creates in your life, prophet of God.

There were the men who were at war against David, and now 400 men came to David and proved to be a reflection of where David was and what God had done to him in the cave. Men who have fought with David now see he is alive and has stood through the test.

Prophet, you will always attract who you are. Look at your life, and you will draw who you are to you. People will come to you, prophet; you do not have to figure it out. God will send them to you. All you have to do is stand there, and those like you will find you in your personal Cave of Adullam. They found David and made David their leader.

Prophet, you earn the right to lead because of your experiences. God takes you through many personal traumas to equip you with what it means to be an element of change in people's lives.

These men left Saul, who had more resources than David, but they could relate to David, which is what is happening in so many of your lives. We must examine David's life to fully understand what is happening to him.

Let's look at his background, which is so seldom looked at. The prophets of today will benefit as they look at the Illegitimate Bastard curse of the prophets.

Prophet, it is a fact that you must allow God to vindicate you while you are in your Cave of Adullam. God will show you to others and open you up to people who want and know there is more. Let's now examine the background of David and see if you can relate to his background.

CHAPTER 2

The Illegitimate Bastard Curse of Prophets

We need to look at some issues with the background of David as we seek to understand why he is a poster child for our development as prophets. We need to understand some history to understand David. This will help us know how we deal with our personal issues.

Let's now look at why we need to reference the illegitimate bastard curse of prophets.

Genesis 6 provides us a reference to what many refer to as a bastard offspring. These are the days of Noah filled with wickedness, and there are references to the sons of God. They are the fallen angels of *Jude 1:6*. They are described as having left their first estate. They came to earth to mate with women.

Their offspring were referred to as bastards. Have you noticed that God's heart was grieved by what was called "the bastard curse on the bloodlines"? While those who were referred to as bastards were not excluded from public worship ordinarily, it is significant that they had no claim to the paternal inheritance or to the standing privileges and discipline of children *(Hebrews 12:7)*.

Now please imagine that some societies also question whether someone conceived out of wedlock would be a bastard if the parents married before the child was born. There is the Jewish law as the word bastard appears in *Deuteronomy 23:3*.

The stigma of being called a bastard is that you shall not enter into the assembly of the Lord. This is ten generations long. There is no entry into the assembly of the Lord. Let me also be clear that the word "bastard" is not exactly equitable to the English word bastard. This was not a joke by no means.

Let's now look at exactly who was a "bastard." Remember this, through the Old Testament, we are referring to a child born of an Israelite father and a heathen or a non-Israelite mother. Now that you have some brief history, look with me at the prominent examples of God's great men and women who had kids who would fit into this category.

These are some of the most prominent prophetic figures who had children from non-Israelites. We see the list of prophets here, which is eye-opening. There is Moses, King David, Abraham, Isaac, and Jacob. Then there is Joseph, King Solomon, and their children were not considered bastards.

Ask the question many have asked, and it is why is a child of a married woman and of a man that is not her husband a bastard? The strangeness is that a man could be married to a woman and have children from other women. These children would not be considered bastards. Let me be clear on this point. A married woman has a child, and it is with a man who is not her husband; the child would be a bastard. The standard was strange and clearly unfair.

This is where we now pick up the life of David and let's look closer. The life of David will apply. David himself is a bastard; he is a child begotten out of unlawful matrimony, an illegitimate child.

David also was the father of a child that was the result of sex outside of marriage. Bathsheba was Uriah's wife when she conceived a child with David. That child was illegitimate. It was a bastard. While the child fits the criteria for being called a bastard, few, if any, had the nerve to call it a bastard. David, by this time in his life, was a prominent and influential leader.

On the other hand, we look at the term, bastard. It is representative of a different idea. The word means someone begotten of a forbidden marriage or by those who cannot marry under the law. The phrase "those born of a forbidden marriage" rather than bastard has also been used.

Forbidden marriages included the list of nations that the Israelites were forbidden to intermingle with, as well as incest and adultery. This is a very serious matter in Jewish law, and it is understood "even to the tenth generation" to mean forever literally.

The union of David and Bathsheba was certainly a forbidden marriage, and therefore, Solomon was seen as a bastard by some despite God's blessing upon his life.

Many believed that a bastard had a curse upon their life. Look at a curse as an expressed wish for adversity or doom. Some have connected misfortune and attached that misfortune to some other entity or person. This can include one or more persons, a generation, a place, or an object. Let us also note that a "curse" may refer to a wish for harm. The infliction will be by any supernatural powers, such as a spell, a prayer, an imprecation, an execration, magic, witchcraft, a natural force, or a spirit. Scripture teaches us about curses, especially when we do wrong with our money and resources.

In many belief systems, reversing or eliminating a curse is called removal or breaking and is often believed to require elaborate rituals or prayers. This is the time David lived in. Some people knew about his life. David himself was affected by his status.

When considering your personal status, can you see issues like this in your culture? You can't ignore this or similar issues in your life. Ignoring your issues will not work now or moving forth. This will not work if you want to grow and develop in your prophetic mantle.

God created man in His image, and fellowship is high on God's agenda, especially for us, His prophets. The bastard curse prevents that fellowship from occurring because the consequence of this curse is that people are not able to come into the congregation of the Lord with a bastard. *Zechariah 9:6* says to us that a bastard shall dwell in Ashdod. Ashdod is a city of Philistia not much more than ten miles from Goliath's hometown.

The bastard curse is very powerful in the carnal sense, yet it is just as powerful in the spiritual sense. We see it today in the lives of prophets who justify their sin in wilderness situations for various reasons, and sin leads to more sin.

The bastard curse is reflected as a ten-generation event. It is an excellent way to say forever. Today it reflects a corrupt perception in the prophetic ministry, with the enemy attempting to discredit and shut you up. This shows up in multiple ways. This work is done to the prophet with personal isolation and torment, family issues, and personal persecution from people of perceived influence.

No other sin in the Bible results in such an enduring curse; consider the ramifications David faced as a small kid. The thought of the day was that death was the only means to eradicate the effects of this curse. Not only was the death of the immediate preparations required to eliminate it, but their entire bloodline had to be purged by death. Can you see how seriously this was looked at?

This was David's world. This is who he was and the environment he grew up in. David had a curse following him. Prophets, can you see David? He had a curse with demonic authority to attempt to interfere with the will of God upon his life.

Does this sound like you, or does it not? Be honest with yourself, prophet. Contemporary, now day prophets should note the life of David and understand that God has allowed you to go through some situations in order to prepare you for service. Can you feel your situation as David felt his?

Now that we have discussed some background of the environment David dealt with, let's look even deeper. Genesis tells us that the bastard curse was Satan's primary tactic of destruction. Satan was busy.

We see his work in Judah's bloodline to David. By corrupting the bloodline, he could keep God's children from developing a close relationship with Him and try to spoil the woman's seed from being born.

Prophets listen closely, as we see this in a lot of the families of prophets. This is why I shared with you that the curse is carnal and spiritual. The prophetic family has its own way of connecting prophets and supporting them to obtain greatness through prophetic development. This is so important.

Today we experience this and realize that prophetic mentorship and a prophetic lineage are not by chance. This is by the divine will of God. This is not by chance, I repeat.

Satan did not know that God arranged a plan, but he had a strategy to destroy the bloodline so thoroughly that it could not produce the seed necessary to defeat him, as spoken by God in *Genesis 3:14-15*.

Let us now connect this with the life of David and see what he went through. David's life is like the life of a few others *(1 Samuel 16:1-13)*. Saul has been the king of Israel by God. God had commissioned the Prophet Samuel to anoint one of Jesse's sons. This son was to be the next king of Israel.

Jesse gathers his sons. Samuel discerns that none of the boys standing before him has been chosen by God. That's the prophetic discernment exercised by Samuel.

Samuel now asks if there are any other sons not there. He is told the youngest, David, is attending the flock. Samuel now wants to see David. He meets David, and now he is appointed as the next king of Israel.

A question to ponder here is why David was not initially included? Was there a compelling reason why David was not invited to be there? Some say David was omitted because he was the youngest and doing all the work. That was not the case when you look at *Psalm 51:5*.

Psalm 51:5 gives us insight into the life of David. David writes his thoughts in the aftermath of his adulterous affair with Bathsheba. Notice he writes about his mother, and he says, "Behold I was birthed in sin and in sin my mother conceived me."

We all know of the sinful nature that plagues all mankind. The Garden of Eden, with the sin of Adam and Eve, is the cause. We need to look at the Word. David says, "in sin, my mother conceived me." David is speaking about his mother and identifying his birth as sinful. Do you understand what David is saying?

Let's examine this, David is saying his mother committed adultery, and he, David, was the byproduct of this infidelity. David's mother was a wife who committed adultery. David speaks of his mother as she brought huge shame upon Jesse and his family.

He is also saying he is an illegitimate son of Jesse and this has affected his life. This would affect your life also. Again I ask you to look at David and look at your issues. Is there a prophet who can relate to this? Maybe your situation is not necessarily biological, but it is spiritual.

You know there is not a connection there like others with your family, or some of you may be dealing with this in your ministries or churches, as your gift has separated you. Some look and refer to you or make you feel like a black sheep, but God has special plans for you *(Jeremiah 29:11)*.

Now you should understand why David was not initially included. The reality of a dark secret becomes clear as David was not a true son of Jesse. Dark secrets are a norm in the life of many prophets.

Let's look at this as God included David as part of Jesse's family. Keep in mind this is how Jesus was considered a son of Joseph. The conception was through the Holy Spirit.

Prophets, you must understand that you're a part of God's family, so important that you have been designated as His instrument of divine communication *(Amos 3:7)*. This is real talk.

Let's now look at an even deeper angle concerning David and his personal life. David also refers to his mother in *Psalm 69:8*. David opens his heart and says, "I have become estranged from my brothers." He feels he is an alien to his mother's sons. Prophets, can you relate? You are different, but God has a plan for your life; don't despair.

David was ostracized and estranged from his own family and was considered an alien or an outcast by his brothers. Notice how David refers to his brothers as his mother's sons, not his father's, indicating they shared the same mother but not the same father. Prophet, can you relate to this?

David uses the Hebrew word for estranged, as he refers to an individual who has come from "adultery." He is that individual who has come from another man.

The Hebrew word "mamzer" means he knows he is a bastard or illegitimate child. This is how David and many of us as prophets today feel as we have been through these types of issues in our life.

Our problems today stem from the fact that many of our prophets have not recovered from these issues or never recognized them. In *Psalm 69:21*, David describes mistreatment as he was not included in regular family activities such as meals. He speaks of them giving him gall for food and vinegar instead of water or their favorite punch. Gall, if you don't know, is a bitter plant like worm wood. Overall it appears the brothers made David's life miserable.

David's life was not a life of family love. David, because he is different, he's looked upon as an illegitimate bastard. David's relationship with Jesse is one of understanding as we see no conflict as Jesse gets David to take food to his brothers fighting the Philistines.

David shows up at the Israel army camp; you immediately see the animosity between David and his brothers *(1 Samuel 17: 28-29)*. This conflict between David and his half-brothers strongly indicates his prophetic-like status of being different. The relationship he had with his brothers is a mirror of what many of us have with certain family, friends, or acquaintances.

Prophets, look at *Psalm 69* for yourself and see the misery David endured growing up. Because of his mother's sin, David's childhood was full of loneliness and rejection.

In *Psalm 69:3,* he speaks of hours spent crying because of the rejection. How many of us today have been rejected and not developed because of rejection? In *Psalms 69:4,* He explains his frustration of being punished for a sin he did not commit; it was his mother's sin, and he became the object of mockery as the drunkards sang about his plight *(v 26).*

David's young days should convince you of the need for mentorship and fellowship. It should serve as a living warning of what happens to those dealing with the sins of your previous generations.

Psalms 69:11-12 says David's treatment was a pity to hear. He says his clothing was sackcloth, my clothing. He was a joke to his brothers and even the drunks and beggars of the area. Welcome to the world of the emerging prophet trying to find himself.

What was particularly hurtful was those who "sit at the gate" used him as an example of what happens when people sin. "Sit at the gate" refers to the city elders who sat at the gates and made judgments on cases. Every prophet who is relevant, or even if people suspect you may be relevant, you have been judged or will be judged. You must understand this.

Your critics or haters are allowed in your life for a reason; you must understand how to manage them.

In *Psalm 69:19-20,* David pours out his heart. Here again, we see the heart of David. He speaks of his reproach, his shame, and his dishonor. What his mom has done has caused him to be shamed.

All my adversaries are before You. Reproach has broken my heart. He feels everybody knows, and the reality of him being sick is real. David said he looked for sympathy, but there was none, and he found none for comforters.

David teaches us that there is a reality in being considered an outsider, black sheep, or different. Many of you should relate to this.

John 9:2-3 echoes the Jewish belief that children could be punished for the sins of their parents. This is seen as the disciples after stumbling upon a blind man. They then asked Jesus if he was being punished for his parent's sins or his own.

Prophets understand how serious this is as many of you have been despised and rejected by family and humiliated by those in his home town; God saw David's heart and how he responded to the rejection and the ugliness that filled his childhood and chose this boy as the next king of Israel. Now the question must be asked, do you want to be God's prophet and deal with the ridicule, unfair, and unreasonable critiques of your life?

Rejection, bitterness, and rebellion are very noticeable, especially in a prophet or a person under the bastard curse. The conception results from the spirit of lust, not love. Demons of lust will follow all children of the line involved.

True love involves protecting and providing, things not present when the child is conceived. This is what God does for His prophets who will listen and foster a relationship with Him.

Multiple demons will appear, follow the prophet and try to gain entrance. Many now-generation prophets, in their families, have been conceived as bastards unwanted by either of the parents. The reality of that statement will surprise many. Look at our issues today and the results, and question why?

Some prophets have excessive problems with rejection, lust, anger, hate, envy, and jealousy, getting along with co-workers, sexual impurity, sexual lust, alcohol and drug use, fascination with crime, the occult, and witchcraft are noted in many cases. Spirits of Jezebel, Ahab, automatic failure, and self-hatred may be present in the lives of some prophets.

Sure, you may see this in others who are not prophetic. We understand this, but let's look at the fact that we are specifically assigned, according to *Amos 3:7*, as the mouthpieces of God.

Some inactive and undeveloped prophetic gifts are subject to being unsettled, irresponsible, and have difficulty in maintaining church membership or staying in a marriage. Not all prophets are affected like this, but many are. I am sure you could list other issues to add here.

The "vagabond curse" (wandering) is very common in prophets also. The prophet may function in either of two extremes – confrontational or withdrawn (refusing to handle situations).

Just as some children, conceived out of wedlock, know in the womb that they are not wanted if abortion is attempted or considered. The "spirit of murder" can enter at this time.

Some prophets become hardened in their hearts and have difficulty in receiving love and friendship and in giving these things to others. Some prophets will choose a mate who will not share or receive love but operate in a spirit of coldness.

David's household was cursed with the sword, his wives were taken by others, and rape occurred in the family. Adultery, murder, abortion, incest, wandering, insecurity, and sexual sins, all these may arise from and out of the bastard curse. The Holy Spirit will reveal if this curse exists in your family line as a generational curse. Should there be such a curse in your family, make sure you read and confess *Leviticus 26:40-46*.

Prophets, this bastard curse is broken with deep-seated repentance and God's forgiveness of this sin. Prophets, break the bastard curse, cast out the bastard-connected demons, and pray for healing of the broken spirit, hurt, wounds, rejection, and shame. Accept God's love and His total forgiveness. Renew your mind in the Lord. Read the following *Rom. 12:1-2, Lev.26:40, and Hosea 4:6.*

Prophet, this illegitimate bastard curse is rampant world-wide and is affecting prophets of all races. It seeks to destroy the lives of the prophets. God will bring judgment upon those who continue this practice. God will forgive. This is why we must set goals and work to obtain them.

We must move forward and not sit and brew. Goal setting is necessary for the prophetic, especially as we talk about moving away from curses in our lives.

My question is, are you a prophet who will set goals.? The curse of the illegitimate bastard can be broken. Jesus is ready and willing to help those prophets caught in this curse and its destruction. Prophets remember that a relationship with God is everything! This is why you want to set Goals. Let's now discuss visualization. Like David, we must set goals.

CHAPTER 3

Prophets Setting Goals

Philippians 3:14 says I press toward the mark for the prize of God's high calling in Christ Jesus. The Word mark here is used to describe the goal. For all prophets, we should have a goal to get closer to God, and for prophets, it is essential to be close to God to allow His gifts within us to flourish.

As prophets, we have an awesome gift that energizes our prophetic gift called visualization, which is the formation of mental images of communication with God. Some are seen, and some are heard. This is a gift that David had, and he used it at will. Prophets have and continue to use this gift to set life goals.

Visualization will vary with each prophetic gift. When we study prophets like David, we see they employed visualization. We see their utterance spoken and actions were of what they knew to be accurate, the Word of God. This is a relationship with God that has to be tested to be effective.

We see that David was effective in his gifting. As the now generation prophets of today, as we practice visualizing our dreams as already complete, we can rapidly accelerate on what we need to do with the vision God has given us to accomplish His purposes which should be our goals. Dreams without goals are only dreams.

The Visualization process was employed in Elijah's ministry in 2 different ways.

Visualization:1

It activates our creative subconscious, generating creative ideas to achieve our goal. Our minds stay open to what God is showing us. The prophet Elijah continuously employed this concept except after dealing with and defeating the prophets of Baal. Even after Elijah ran after his encounter with the demonic servant of Jezebel, his situation allowed his thinking to more readily perceive and recognize what he needed to achieve his goal.

Visualization:2

It activates the law of attraction and internal motivation. Thereby drawing into your life the people, resources, and circumstances, you will need to achieve your goals.

Think of David on the mountain with the sheep and how he looks at his situation. He is looking at something totally opposite to how he will mature. Imagine the future king of Israel using visualization to cope with his situation as a future leader.

Consider his history and consider standing with his family. Allow him to look as we look at ourselves today. The future king of Israel is moving sheep dung as he cares for his stepfather's sheep. He was in an environment where he may not have made it out without visualization. David was able to set a goal and stay focused.

As today's generation of prophets, we need to set goals for our lives. We need to learn four powerful basic facts necessary. These were what the biblical prophets used, and they achieved greatness in God with these facts. These four undeniable facts are essential for prophets to set effective goals. We, the now generation prophets, must know the following without compromise.

Biblical prophets considered themselves servants of God, vehicles through whom God Himself spoke. They had confidence in their relationship with God. In *Exodus 7:1*, God says to His servant Moses, 'I have made you like God to Pharaoh.' Moses, the essence of God's example of a prophet in the Old Testament, shows us how to speak with an authority not his own.

Prophets came to their work as the result of an experience of a divine call. The word they spoke was God's Word and not their own. There was no evidence that they simply felt permitted to display. They considered themselves required by God to do what they did; that's confidence.

They considered the content of their message directly from God. They were the voice of God, who knew His Word and spoke and acted on it. The prophets were God's covenant people, and they offered His Word to the world.

God's Word was related to the original covenant He had given through Moses. God raised the prophets to bring the people back to obedience to the original covenant.

The Old Testament prophets simply did not see themselves as innovators. They considered themselves occupying a divinely appointed office, correcting illegal beliefs and practices by divine word. When the prophets are called to denounce Israel or other nations, their attack was a crime against the covenant of God.

These crimes range from religious-doctrinal, that is crimes of heterodoxy *(Hos. 2: 4-13; Ezek. 8:6-16).* To have such a ministry was sometimes considered the equivalent of treason *(Am. 7: 10-11).*

Today in some circles, we see the same thing. God's Word was always the standard of correction. We see the prophet Amos as he answers the complaint that his message was negative, but he offers no response.

His appointment to office was God's doing. He knew it and expressed it as he answered King Amaziah. He tells him it is what God says *(Amos. 7: 14-17)*. They understood their message; the prophets were fully aware and conscious of what was happening around them.

The prophets are keenly aware of what their message can or will result in. The prophet Jonah flees at first from his divinely appointed task because he understands his cry against Nineveh might bring change. He serves as a vehicle for Assyrian repentance.

He does not think the Assyrian people deserve to hear him speak. He is a student of his own personal arrogance. Despite his arrogance, he knew what the Word of God would do.

There are eight facts. Prophets need to understand and embrace as they set goals for their ministry.

Understand these eight facts in your process of prophetic goal setting. Here are some guidelines to address as we set our prophetic goals. Let us look at David as we look at these eight facts.

1.Determine why you want to excel in this area.

Knowing what vision God has given, can help you stay focused on it in moments of difficulties and doubt. Usually, when we start working on a new project, we are overly excited and super motivated. But those feelings don't last forever. They typically come and go. Did you notice that David was almost always focused and calm in all areas of his life?

2. Determine how you want to achieve your goal and what will change in your life to achieve your goal?

How will it affect your relationship? You must believe you can achieve your goal despite what you see or feel.

If you start by doubting your possibilities, one thing will happen for sure. You will fail. A non-believing prophet is an unfocused prophet. This was David to a tee. He was super focused, and everybody around him knew it.

A known fact of what you expect, will eventually manifest itself in your reality. On the contrary, if you really believe you can do it, you will start seeing all the possibilities to make it happen, and you will have more courage and energy to achieve your goals.

Remember how God kept telling Joshua to be strong and be of good courage? It is not always easy to have that kind of faith. This will speak significantly to your relationship with God.

3. Analyze your starting point.

You know where you want to go. Prophets need to be honest when analyzing where they are, as it will allow them to understand what they need to do. Again, be honest with yourself. This is not the moment to allow your ego to sabotage your efforts.

Whatever your goal is, thoroughly analyze your strengths and weaknesses in this area. David did this in his analysis of who he was; remember Goliath.

4. Identify the obstacles.

Prophets, you will encounter difficulty on your way to achieving your desired outcome. But don't let that discourage you. Everybody who has achieved great goals in their lives had to overcome obstacles. Prophets, it is hard to imagine anyone in scripture with more obstacles than David.

We, as prophets, are no different; we are the spiritual poster children for hard times. Think of what an obstacle for you could be. Knowing what the worst-case scenario can be, allows you to be prepared, so you will know exactly what to do if the obstacle does appear. Again, nothing replaces our faith to overcome.

5. Determine the additional knowledge and skill you need.

You have a goal. Now ask yourself, prophet, why this goal is yet to be a reality. Always remember the need and development of new skills and knowledge to achieve your goals. This is where the School of The Prophet, Prophetic Conferences, and Revivals are essential.

These types of prophetic watering holes are our continuing education. Identify them and use them. Understand what you need to become relevant in the exponent of your gift. David demonstrated this by surrounding himself with the Philistines for safety and balance. Stop thinking that you know it all and start reading, attending, and doing the necessary work.

6. Determine the people you'll need.

Prophets, you will be wise to know that at more than once, you will need help from somebody. Identify key people for your success. Prophet, you need to know who can teach you what you need to know. Who can help you stay focused and motivated?

Once you have that list, start working on relationships with these people. Offer them your help first. On his way to becoming King, David learns a valuable lesson as the future king. He teaches his men a valuable lesson also.

Offer yourself, sow seeds and be consistent. This was David, for sure. Don't expect them to help you if you are unwilling to do the same for them. Be genuine and honest. Do not use anybody for your goals but create genuine relationships beneficial for both of you.

7. Make a plan.

You have probably heard the saying: what does not get planned doesn't get done. How true have we found this in our prophetic walks? Having a plan for achieving your goal is essential to your success. Without it, how will you know what to work on? Resources like time and energy are priceless and irreplaceable, and they must be put to the right use.

Make a plan. This is your road map. Be flexible. Observe change and understand you may need to adjust your plan more than once. Be open for it. Planning itself is an essential part of achieving goals. David's plan was God's, and he was trusted to do just that.

8. Never give up.

This is what made David who he was. The key to achieving your goal is persistence. No matter how much talent you have or how gifted you are, if you do not persist, you might just give up right before your big breakthrough.

Don't let any failures discourage you. You already know that obstacles will happen. Whenever they do, work on them and keep going forward. Once you decide you want to achieve a goal, make a decision never to give up.

Finally, there are three foundational goals that all prophets need to pursue to elevate themselves and increase themselves in every area of their life and ministry to accomplish the goals that God has given them the vision for.

The three irreplaceable goals are to:

1. Study diligently.
2. Pray earnestly.
3. Serve willingly.

First, **study diligently.** *John 5:39* tells us to spend time in the scriptures. The answers to eternal life are there. A study of the Word of God will build our testimonies and the testimonies of our family members.

Children today face many challenges and many voices. The world wants us not to pursue God, especially when the world's pleasures are always flashed before us.

Those of you reading this book should realize the following. You need a firm foundation in the gospel of Jesus Christ. This is the foundation of truth and living righteously. Our kids are susceptible to worldly influences. It is our responsibility to fortify and protect them.

2 Timothy 7-8 tells us God has not raised us up to be afraid. We, as His prophets, will operate in power, love, and a sound mind. Prophet, we must not be ashamed of the testimony of our Lord. Again, study diligently. Did you notice that David studied and prayed alone with the sheep on the mountain?

Pray earnestly. *1 Thessalonians 5:16-18 says, "Pray without ceasing. Give thanks in all circumstances."* We can offer these as being very unique times. We can receive the needed blessings and support through earnest and heartfelt prayer. This is required to make our way in this sometimes difficult and challenging journey again; pray earnestly.

Serve willingly. David's servitude speaks for itself. Look at him on the mountain as a small boy to his time as King of Israel. We see him serve in a multitude of ways.

As a prophet, your influence ranges far beyond yourself. Prophet, what you do touches others worldwide in ways we often don't imagine. God will always surround service opportunities.

Sometimes as a prophet, you recognize opportunities that you may feel somewhat overwhelmed. Where do you begin? How can you do it all? From all the needs you observe, how do you choose where and how to serve?

Sometimes small acts of service are all that is required to lift and bless another:

- A question concerning a person's family
- Quick words of encouragement
- A sincere compliment
- A small note of thanks
- A brief telephone call

Prophets, we must be observant and aware. God will send things for us to take action on. Through God's promptings that come to us, we can accomplish much good. Sometimes, of course, more is needed.

The ability to serve with honor is evident as we have looked at David in the aspect that he dealt with family issues and was still able to focus on working with honor in difficult situations. David did not run from drama.

I discussed this briefly in chapter 1, and now in chapter 4, I will discuss another attribute of David: his honor. Prophets, just like David, we must exhibit and practice honor.

I will explain more about this in the next chapter. Prophet, by now, you should have seen David in the Cave of Adullam; it was the time for him to realize some things about himself. His life looked one way, and things were another.

As David does, you and I showcase a desire to be excellent with a willingness to help. I, like David, seek the graciousness to give that comes from a heart filled with love. Serve willingly. You will develop the seed of access in your life called honor.

David shows us his internal attitude about himself; we refer to it as a prophetic honor, and you and I must realize and understand it.

CHAPTER 4

Prophetic Honor

When we think of honor, it recognizes someone in a position of authority or significant influence. This is true, but for a prophet, it is even more. In chapter 1, we discussed David, who could have run but did not. David trusted and honored God in the most challenging times of his life.

Do you remember that he was a standard of excellence in a troubled time? This is what Prophetic Honor is about. What David had on the inside was prophetic honor.

Prophetic honor for a prophet is an internal attitude of respect and reverence. This has a foundation of giving earned attention with obedience. The prophet Isaiah was wise as he reflected on honor and its seriousness.

Isaiah 29:13 reflects on honor today as it is referenced with the lips of flattering words, yet there is no foundation of honor in the heart. That is incomplete, honor.

Incomplete honor is no honor; it is simply lip service for the prophet of God, who honors God through their servitude. The granting of honor in the life of a prophet is essential to a prophet's life. We discussed this in the previous chapter of Prophets Setting Goals. This includes honoring the position of earthly authority.

There is a clear false humility throughout the Body of Christ. We have mature Christians who will disregard men and women of God by failing to honor them all because they believe it is unimportant to do so.

This is true of the prophetic. Do we not see God honors His prophets? God does expect His people to do the same. One crucial issue is that many have not been taught to honor prophets because the 5-fold ministry was never a part of the church or ministry they grew up in.

So the question is, why would anyone honor a prophet? Two very good reasons come to mind.

1. *Amos 3:7* echoes the high-value God puts on His prophets. God does nothing unless He reveals what He intends to do to His servants, the prophets.

2. *Matthew 10:41* also clarifies that you will prosper when you receive and honor a prophet. Can you receive one of God's prophets properly and inherit and receive a prophet's reward? *(2 Chronicles 20:20)* The Word of God will establish you.; believe His prophets, and you shall prosper."

Every prophet needs to identify the prophet in their life and learn how to honor that prophet. The process of honor has been greatly misunderstood in many of our lives. Many prophets have sought the reception of honor; the truth is, it is not an experience to be sought.

Honor is earned through character and discipline. This describes David. No, he was not perfect, but look at his life, and you will see his character and discipline, even when he was wrong.

Luke 14:11 tells us that honor is given to the humble, those who have the character of humility, and they are exalted. Prophets know that when honor comes from others because of their position or status as a prophet, it is not to be taken for granted. You should merit honor through your Godlike character as a prophet or seer.

Who remembers Jesus as He returns home and the people are so excited, and within the same breath, they are frustrated. We all should be able to relate to this. Look at the dishonor in the world today.

There is an overflow of dishonor in the Body of Christ. There is so much dishonor in the prophetic community we choose to ignore it, hoping it will go away. The spirit of dishonor is running wild.

Today we see prophets dishonored, and we choose to dishonor each other. In *Matthew 13:57,* Jesus says that a prophet is not without honor except in his own country. Notice that Jesus did not do many works there. As a matter of fact, He did very little mighty work because of their unbelief.

When honor is not shown, the release of a dishonor spirit rests upon one's life. Prophets are not immune to this; it is an invisible barrier that will constantly stop the blessings of God. Dishonor will be smoother and breed unbelief. Teaching someone to honor is a lost art today.

Today, we see dishonor released by our words, deeds, and actions toward others, and it stops us from building the relationships needed for growth. Dishonor in the prophetic creates a reality that shuts down what God has for you from someone you may have dishonored. Jesus was dishonored, and He did no mighty works. Dishonor stopped the blessings Jesus had for the people.

You're a prophet, and your spirit of honor is projected through your open reception of those you encounter. David had a life that he lived with integrity. Even when he was wrong, he still was honored by Uriah.

Your level of prophetic honor is displayed through your reception of others. People who encounter you also as a prophet are put in a situation either to honor or reject you.

You must understand that their reception of you as a prophet reflects their ability to receive the blessings God has for them through the mantle upon your life. Stop getting mad with people who do not know how to receive you.

They are relating to you, the prophet, at their comfort level. This is why when we look at David, we see him know and operate in a level of honor that many of us need to learn.

This is the level of intellect they know and chooses to operate in. We get mad, upset, and fall out with people because they do not understand prophetic honor. This is why you, the prophet, have to be extra careful, as you will encounter people you are not fond of, nor do you care or expect to receive of them. The prophet must remember to honor those in positions of authority, whether we like them or not.

This is why whomever you honor, you get access to, and whomever you dishonor, becomes shut off to you. These are the choices we make in our lives daily. What is your scope of visualization showing you that will make you dishonor someone?

The critical point to realize is that reception matters. How do we receive and honor in our house and in another prophet's house matters? Receiving a prophet is a serious manner to God. He will assure his servants get the prophet's reward.

Prophet, while the word is accurate, it does not necessarily mean your feelings are valid. Here again, David provides the example, remembering his brothers seeing him being anointed as the next king. The word was accurate, and their feeling obviously was not.

What does that mean? Get your emotions and feelings out of the way, and receive them in the office of the prophet, with the prophet's authority. Your personal feelings have nothing to do with where God has raised them. You can be upset, mad, angry, and feel you have been done wrong, but you put yourself in a dishonored place with God.

David honored Saul, even when Saul hunted him like an animal. In *1 Samuel 24:6*, David, who could have killed Saul, told his men, I will not touch the Lord's Anointed. Many of us today must keep working to achieve that level of honor.

Who has done you wrong, and you still honored them because it was the right thing to do? Remember, Saul was in a position of authority. The honor was in David; it was a part of who he was, his character, and his integrity.

Today, as we look in the prophetic community, there is another very important point, and that is we have to make a distinction that God has raised them up and not them naming themselves a prophet, apostle, or seer without any due process, and allowing someone in authority to elevate them and not themselves.

Honor will release mighty works and miracles within one's life. The prophetic community needs a culture of honor if we are to fulfill our destiny within the mandate of God.

There will never be a day when we will agree on everything, but we should be able to honor and respect, despite our differences. When we see how that has worked so far, we all know we have work to do.

We are to give honor where honor is due. Let's look again at the Body of Christ, and we all know there are so many self-appointed titles and offices. You may know and not agree with that. Most of us do not, but that still does not give us the right or authority to disrespect anyone.

Prophetic honor is internal, and it is not a feeling based on disagreement but on character and values that a prophet has developed internally. Prophetic honor acts within the prophet; even if one disrespects the prophet, the prophet must know that they must be true to the prophet's honor.

The prophet cannot allow dishonor to affect what God has given them in their life. Dishonor will affect every area of your life. In *Numbers 12,* we see Prophetess Miriam and Prophet Aaron, who disapproved of Moses' wife.

Moses, a recognized leader and prophet of the people, married an Ethiopian woman, and his older brother and older sister did not like it. His siblings verbally attack him. Both of them are prophets. They are anointed of God, yet both verbally attack Moses, their little brother.

God heard them speak this. This is the spirit of dishonor at work. Moses' two older siblings are jealous and can't receive Moses. Notice that everyone around Moses honored him but not his own family. They dishonored the chosen one of God.

God now speaks to both of them but speaks to them of his relationship with Moses and the favor upon their lives because of Moses. He tells them that Moses, His prophet is special to Him, and now we see leprosy come to Miriam. God isolated Miriam for seven days with leprosy.

Leprosy is contagious, and now people have another reason to stay away from Miriam. Leprosy causes one to lose feelings, just like the spirit of dishonor causes one to lose feelings for God. This was serious, as God looks at this.

In *Genesis 9,* we see Noah and Ham and how Ham acted when he saw Noah drunk and naked. He told his brother what he saw of Noah.

Ham did not have a spirit of honor in his life. This was his dad, and you see how he acted. This type of behavior is why there is a lack of prophetic honor in the prophetic community today.

We see this today with prophets who look for the drama and shortcomings, or they may be exposed. This is a test for many of us as to what we need to develop.

We will gossip rather than pray. We will dishonor rather than honor because it is easier than working on ourselves in our weak areas. Prophetic honor, when developed, allows a prophet to fulfill their destiny as mandated by God.

Let's look at the facts: Noah was dishonored and used mighty by God as Ham saw fit to have him dishonored. As Noah prophesied, he spoke to Ham and told him his son Canaan would be cursed. Prophet, we see generational cursing because of the spirit of dishonor.

If you do not have a prophet, ask yourself why? Why do I not believe it? Why do I not trust God or His servants? Why do I always look for what is wrong so that I can constantly dishonor God's servants? Have this conversation with yourself. Ask yourself the question?

Consider this wisely that you need a prophet in your life? But how does that happen? Trust God that the person will do the following that He sends into your life.

1. The prophet will speak life into your dark areas. This will be in prayer and conversation.

2. The prophet will always have a prophetic agenda to bring you to the next level!

3. The prophet has a burden for your spiritual, emotional, and financial growth! Your sowing into that prophet's life is not by accident. It is by divine intervention. This is called establishing a financial covenant. That covenant connects you to the prophet's reward.

These 3 points combined in the work of a prophet in your life will lift you out of your Egypt and into your Promised Land. This is a work that can't be dishonored and does not work on your personal clock; it works on God's clock.

Please do yourself a great favor and honor your prophet. Honor, value, and respect them! The honor that the prophet walks in will be the foundation of prophetic honor within your life.

This is critical as there needs to be an agreement with people in your life. I want to take this to another level as we will look at the power of agreement, the story of Achan, in the next chapter.

The church itself is built on the foundations of apostles and prophets! No spiritual movement, church, or anything God builds in His kingdom is ever started without the apostolic and prophetic mandate!

If you don't have someone who speaks with a prophetic mandate over your life, begin praying, position yourself spiritually and discern as the Lord begins to bring someone into your life! You need to be in agreement with someone.

Therefore, we rejoice that we are no longer strangers and foreigners. We are members of the household of God. We all lean on the foundation of the apostles and prophets. Jesus is the chief cornerstone *(Ephesians 2:20)*. This is an agreement, and keep in mind how dishonor separates us from agreement.

Remember, the fivefold ministry is a gift to the Body of Christ, and you will be incredibly blessed when you learn to honor the servants of God in your life. Live a life of honor.

A spirit of dishonor will dismantle your family. This chapter was important to show the prophet that, as you find yourself in your Adullam like David. He saw honor return to his life in the way of his peers. Honor has a cousin called agreement, and now we must discuss agreement.

CHAPTER 5

Prophetic Agreement, Did You Find Your Achan?

What is an agreement, and why is it essential to prophets? Consider this; an agreement is the harmony of opinion, action, or character. The agreement is also an arrangement as to a course of action. This would be vital to the life of David. Also, in business, we see an agreement as a contract duly binding and legally enforceable.

In the prophetic ministry, we see that prophetic agreement is the coming together of prophets or prophetic people for a course of action to glorify God. The Cave of Adullam is the birth of an agreement between David and his men.

There are events like the school of the prophet, a prophetic conference, or a celebration of prophetic ministry that would demonstrate the harmony of prophets praying and having the same character for the purposes of God.

This would also include a prophetic move. We need to note that this is despite individual differences; the bigger picture is for the pursuit of the will of God. You may feel like this is an issue in the Body of Christ today, and it is.

Acts 15 shares a classic example of agreement and its importance. Men who came down from Judaea to teach the Gentiles. The problem is what they taught. The point of contention was simple.

They wanted the Gentiles to be circumcised after the manner of Moses; ye cannot be saved. This spurred much discussion. There is Paul and Barnabas who disagreed, and now it is determined that they, along with other men, should go to Jerusalem to the apostles and elders to inquire about this question.

Acts 15 features different positions. One issue is whether they should obey the law, and the other is how their obedience should be implemented. Here we have new Gentile converts who were not well versed in the matters of the law.

The nation of Israel was divided into two kingdoms. There were the Northern and Southern Kingdoms. Israel was repeatedly disobeying God. They did not keep His laws, statutes, and judgments.

Then there is the hard-cold reality. It was tough for Jewish Christians to accept that Gentiles, who became Christians, could be brought into the church as "equal partners" without first coming through the law of Moses. Can you see the pockets of agreement and not a broad level of agreement?

This reminds me of today: the lack of agreement in the Body of Christ. Think about this. The reality of working with prophets is that it is hard for some prophets to accept other prophets as they have different ways and different norms. This is due to mainly culture and lineages.

Sometimes prophets and people in general in the Body of Christ will pass a negative judgment on sometimes a group of prophets or all prophets just because of how they were raised in ministry. Have you ever seen someone negative of prophets because of something that happened to them or their beliefs?

Think about David now and realize how he was seen as ascending to be king of all of Israel and surrounding areas on his third anointing. They saw him one way, and God saw him another way.

Notice the same issue here with Paul and Barnabas' missionary endeavors. They were raising churches without bringing them under the Law of Moses. The Jewish establishment was livid.

This is why a deposited experience is so important. We see that Paul and Barnabas had seen God work. The work was so powerful through the Gentiles that they would not abandon it quickly. They were not moved or deterred by what was said.

Often, a prophet or even someone in the Body of Christ does not agree with you as a prophet. The first thing so many of us do is go and play the blame game with them. We all know this game; we tell you one thing but do another, especially behind your back, such as falling out with you.

Paul and Barnabas are now on assignment to have the matter settled. They go to Jerusalem to have the subject put to rest. The apostles and elders were to resolve it. The issue was an issue of agreement. This was about following Jesus.

This effort of Paul and Barnabas found plenty of other Christians who rejoiced at what God had done among the Gentiles. This contrasts with certain men from Judea.

What's funny is that many of the Jewish Christians had been Pharisees. The Pharisees were renowned for their high regard for the law and scrupulous observance.

In summary, we see that what was lost was that Paul and Barnabas would not allow the pagans to merely "add" Jesus to their pantheon of Roman gods. The standard was to cut loose other gods and praise and worship the true God.

Even the Pharisees had to learn how to do the same thing. Once we see agreement, like the Jews and Gentiles, we can see a move of God. For the prophets today, this is difficult to achieve, as well as other 5-fold ministry offices. The agreement is critical as we go from the known to the unknown, meaning the supernatural.

Moving in the prophetic ministry as we are to be the exponent of signs, wonders, and supernatural miracles from God. The devil knows that nothing will be impossible when prophets come together and agree. The devil also knows that where you go in your ministry and who you come into absolute divine agreement with has a bearing on your destiny.

Do you ever wonder why today's prophets fall out with each other at the drop of a leaky faucet? They will say they agree, but they never really agreed. Usually, there is no mediation, only someone gets mad, and then they go their separate ways. The rumors start, and the prophetic community is weakened because we have those immature gifts that want to bud before their time.

Then they create a story for self-fulfillment, self-esteem, and self-elevation. The goal was to make themselves feel better about their inability to understand God's tool of prophetic agreement.

Look around you and see who you're in agreement with; it is a sign of your destiny. Consider Ruth and Naomi, Elijah and Elisha, or even Timothy and Paul. God has invested your destiny in the divine covenant relationships you associate with.

Yes, agreement; prophetic agreement is critical. The goal of the prophetic agreement is reflected in *Malachi 3:10* represents our goal of agreement as prophets and fivefold ministry gifts. Agreeing with God brings the prophets to this place of overflow, where there will be no place to store all their blessings. Are you there yet?'

We all know about *Malachi 3:8,* but do we agree with God? Agreement with God's Word will have us bring our tithes into the storehouse, and God will give us an overflow.

The reality is that we all have room, which leads to the question of why we have room. Remember, this is about agreement. We should not if we are doing what God has said in His Word, and we should be the receipt of the benefit.

Prophet, we are missing this because we don't understand the power of prophetic agreement. How does the prophet understand this? In *Deuteronomy 5:29,* we see God's Word say if they had "such" a heart to fear Me. This would afford them to keep the commandments.

Keeping the commandments will always make things well with family and their children. Does your heart open up to the agreement, Prophets? God is speaking to us in symbolism, and the message is we are not in the agreement we think we are in.

Consider this from the Word of God. One chases a thousand, and two can chase 10,000. God says when you agree with His divine purposes, He will give you supernatural favor and abundance so you will have more than you have ever had.

Look at a marriage and the blessings of this principle. As long as the devil gets in between your marriage, you will function only on the thousand level and miss the opportunity for the supernatural level as God is a God of agreement. This is a message for all of us in the prophetic.

As a prophet, when you can't get along with anyone, falling out with people at the mention of the word itself, you will always labor for not enough; you're going to be broke, busted, and disgusted as you function on a level that God never intended for you to build your work on. All this because you don't understand agreement.

The inability to come to an agreement, especially a prophetic one, is dangerous. Look at *Deuteronomy 32: 29*. If only they were wise, they would understand it and comprehend their fate. We are held accountable, prophets.

Being in agreement is powerful in any endeavor we choose to pursue. Looking into the Body of Christ today, whether it is the prophetic, apostolic, or even the various faiths, being in agreement speaks volumes, especially when we are moving in the will of God.

The enemy does not mind you being in one place together, but the enemy minds you being in agreement. The enemy hates for the prophets to come together spiritually. I have often wondered why getting prophets to come together is so difficult. I am convinced we do not understand the power of agreement.

He is after your agreement. We divide and fall out about anything. Agreement is the power that takes us to the next dimension of God's glory. Agreement will break yokes and bring a whole ministry, state, and nation down for your benefit. Look at Jericho as it fell.

Faith in agreement will bring favor to anyone who believes. Rahab, the harlot, believed, and she was saved from the destruction of Jericho.

She had faith, not because she was saved, but because she had faith to agree with God's Word. This principle will work for whoever chooses to use it.

Prophets of faith will always find themselves in agreement with God and can expect to win in life. They are in it to win it. They know that God is a supplier beyond what they could ask for or even imagine. He is the above-and-beyond God of our lives.

This is why ordinary prophets become extraordinary prophets when we come into agreement. Many will become the beneficiaries of your agreement. Joshua should have whipped AI, but he did not because everyone was not in agreement with him.

God told him he lost the battle because one person failed to honor the covenant. Joshua got the blessing but did not get the corporate blessing because one in the group was not in agreement.

Today too many of us are in agreement with the spirit of survival. God wants to be in agreement with His glorious Spirit of unlimited blessings.

Have you ever asked, where are the blessings God promised me? We, the prophets of the now generation, must agree with God.

Joshua searched for who stole from God; this is what we as leaders must do. We must find out who has blocked your blessings and who is in the way of your blessings.

Aiken has been identified as the one who has robbed God. The accrued ornaments were found in his tent. He was connected to Joshua and blocked the corporate blessing *(Joshua chapter 7).*

Can you picture Aiken and his family being stoned because they were the ones who stopped the corporate blessings of

Israel? They are a blessing where we touch and agree and move mountains.

Who has brought a curse to your life that has stopped the supernatural? Prophets, now search your life as Joshua did. You need revelation not to expose who is the one connected to you that has blocked your agreement with God.

When you find your Aiken, look, and God will give you the strategy to be an overcomer; he will take you to the place of your most significant defeat. God will always bring what you need to fund his ideas. Who you agree with is a powerful thing? Agreement will bring you success because God will give you the strategy.

Learn how to be successful in *Luke 6:38* mode. Look at the process; it says, number one, we give. Once we give, it shall be given unto you; good measure pressed down. There is a shaking and mixing that births overflow. We now have a running over. We qualify for men to give unto us.

The way we measure out is the way it is measured to us. Pressed down, shaken together, and running over because I have agreement in my life. Prophet, do yourself a favor, and tell your peers, friends, and family, "If you're going to be in my life, you must agree with God and His Word." Think about this, those not in agreement with you will not be able to walk with you.

Why is agreement so special? Think about this as we have focused on the development of David and his experience in

Adullam. He is finally able to see. We have covered his background. We have shared this to open his life as a metaphor, especially when your gift takes you to a place you have never known.

Visualization has prepared David and his background and has positioned him for greatness; now, let's explore what happens when you are sent to where you have never been. David was successful, and you will also be successful, read on and follow.

CHAPTER 6

When Your Prophetic Gift Takes You To An Unknown Place

What does it take to move you beyond your traditions and bias concerning the things of God? Have you ever thought that God uses things to bless you that are totally against everything you hold to be true? Can you imagine David dealing with Saul? Saul now comes against him, and David needs to become more familiar with this attitude from Saul.

What happens when God moves or directs you to an unfamiliar place? The place is a situation where you may need formal training. Do you know that you don't know what to expect or do next?

Consider that this will be the place of your blessings. David could be the poster child for this, but let's look at Moses for a minute. Please keep in mind even in this chapter, we are still talking about finding yourself as David did in the cave of Adullam.

In *Exodus 2:11-25,* we see that Moses is a prime example of going to a place he has yet to be mentored to be at. He ends up in the wilderness; this was not what he had expected or planned for his life.

Moses goes from the palace with servants to the smell and grit of the wilderness. Some of us in the prophetic community consider it his punishment, but it's his opportunity, even in the sin of what he has done.

He was not ready to go back to the palace and lead the people of God out of Egypt. This was not his objective, and now the motives of God are at work again in his life. God is sending him to a place where we have not been mentored, and now his faith is on display.

Too many of us in the prophetic get this mixed up. God sends us somewhere, we have not been mentored, and we don't seem to understand it is a faith moment, a time of testing for us.

We believe God is using us rather than developing us. Every prophet must understand that your faith is not empowered in settings with that you are familiar. To not understand this is a fallacy, to say the least.

This is one of our most significant flaws in the prophetic community. Unless I'm familiar with it or I can control the narrative, then I will not want to have anything to do with it.

Faith, for a prophet, is employed in an environment that you are uncomfortable in and with. There are multiple prophets in any of our various circles who want to ascend to levels unknown but never imagined the reality of that in a totally finite imagination.

Imagine if you are a Jew and God sends you to Gentiles. This could not be God, or imagine if you are a Gentile sent to the Jews as a prophet; again, this could not be God. Or could it? Let's look at this today and imagine what if.

You identify as a black prophet, and God sends you to a church with no relevant background in the African American culture. Think about it, and realize that God wants to use you there.

Maybe you identify as a white prophet, and God wants to send you to a Native American church, and you have no cultural identity with that church or its people. Let's consider you identify as a Native American prophet, and God wants to send you to a Hispanic or European Church, and your cultures clearly clash.

Scripturally, we must look at the Book of Amos, prophet Amos, and learn through his reflections. He was a Hebrew prophet sent to minister to Israel, and he was non-Jewish and came in as a total outsider sent by God. This is where God wants to use him at.

The issue is you may want to go to the nations, but you want to go within your own understood structure of how things will be. This is not how God works. David did it, and as a prophet, moving out of your comfort zone means moving forth in God. This is the norm and not the exception.

Look at *Acts chapter 10:5 and Acts 10:24-29:* the story of Peter and Cornelius. Two great men of God were used in the prophetic and the realization of God sending Peter to Joppa. The gift of Peter has sent him to a foreign place, and he is now expected to carry out the agenda of God.

While so many of us are hung up on Peter and his faults, we would be wise to see or even notice our imperfections and where God is sending us that we are unfamiliar with. Can God use you to expand His kingdom, prophet? This means your gift takes you places where you may have to stretch yourself in God to function.

As prophets and seers, we are expected to carry out the motives of God. People who encounter us are the ones who carry the expectations that our titles demand. They have every right to do so.

We live in a world where titles define us. We don't go to the grocery store butcher when we need a heart surgeon. Prophet, prophetess, seer, apostle, and watchman, carry the title, and the expectations are there whether you acknowledge them or not.

So now imagine yourself with a title, and your gift does not measure up to the assignment of it. God now places you in a situation to find yourself, and you want to run or argue with Him.

There is a great divide between what God says and what we understand and do. One fundamental problem here is that when God speaks, many of us must filter whether it is God. This is a real issue.

We often struggle to understand whether it is God, our opinion, or our emotions. Some of us have resigned to the fact our opinion is that of God, also. This is not always the same.

It is reasonable to expect when we are challenged with an assignment that is not of our common norm; we reject it because we cannot control the agenda. You, as a prophet, may want God to expand your agenda, but you do not trust His process. You trust only yours.

Therefore, so many of our today now generation seers and prophets struggle to advance because your gift brings you to a place that your title demands you function in, and there is a loss of connection with you, the prophet, and God.

The loss results from your inability to trust God. This is now the place of disconnection from God and so many of His prophets. This is also where you can least afford it to happen in your life.

The prophet of the now generation is suffering from a lack of God revealing because we lack faith and trust in the God who has gifted us. God knows you, and He knows the level at which you actually do believe and trust.

Think about this prophet because it is serious business. Should you, as the prophet, desire to move forth in God, the prophet must embrace the truths of the next level. When you cannot embrace the truth of the next level, you will never be able to function in it.

Abraham is called to go up the mountain and carry his son as a sacrifice. In *Genesis 22:1-14*, Abraham is called to an assignment that requires supernatural faith. He quickly becomes aware of the fact as he realizes God has told him to sacrifice the son he loves.

The test of his life, ministry, and walk with God is put before Him. He could reject it and declare that it is not the will of God because it is a place he has never been; it is an assignment he has never had.

He, as a father, is not comfortable, but he has an uncanny trust in God. Why could he trust God with his gift, and so many of his now-generation peers could not pass the same test? We serve a God who has no respect of person, and yet that fact is often lost in our emotions and opinions of ourselves.

You want to go from faith to faith and glory to glory; then you will have to understand the reality of the next level of your life that God is bringing you to. Your gift will place you in an experience you have not experienced, and you will find yourself with the dilemma of whether you trust God or you do not.

Here is a nugget to embrace prophet. The truth to the next level is that you will embrace and experience that will require you to let go of some prior truths. Moving to a different level is a different experience.

Has your gift ever taken you to a place where you lacked any experience and had no mental understanding? Has the stress of opportunity caused you to be shy or run away from what you say you were assigned to?

Simply because the reality of change had you not sure if it was God or not. But you did not trust God in the process He had you in. This is a prophetic process of development that every seer will experience.

Go back to *Acts 10,* which shows the experience of Cornelius, a Gentile, and Peter, a Jew. God tells Cornelius that his prayers and giving had been noticed.

He shows him through a vision that he is taking him to a place he has never been. He teaches the lesson of walking by faith and not by sight.

This lesson is for us all as God gives the vision but not the details. The details are revealed in the trusting, so faith is needed. After the dream, he invites all his servants to come over. He now sends for Peter, and he obeys God's directive. God speaks to Cornelius, a gentile, and says all this.

God is also speaking to Peter in a dream. He dreams about animals coming down from heaven, and the voice says that Peter should sley and eat the animals. The animals, however, have been declared unsuitable for eating.

Remember that this is a dream from God, and he is telling Peter to eat specific things, but he does not want to as he disputes what God is telling him to do. Understand that Peter does not want to experience what he has never done before. He does not trust his dream to come from God or the word to be of God.

He declares that the Word of God has put him in place of being a man who has never eaten any of the meats.

God tells Peter that He has cleaned what He wants him to eat, and Peter does not trust it. Something that was forbidden by law comes from Heaven for Peter to eat. God called it unclean, and now He is calling it clean.

We should know it is what God says it is, so we now see a principle of God practiced that we, as prophets, must accept. What was called unclean in Leviticus is now called clean by God in Acts. The reality is that one Word from God will change your life. One Word from God will turn your life around.

David believed, and as a prophet, you must believe that all you need is a Word from God. This applies no matter what our past may be or who we used to be; one Word from God has changed us and turned us around, and now we, the prophets of God, are changed by one Word from God.

We have that same word that will move us into a new arena, platform, and level that many in your life may not be able to accept. They are the ones who have a vision of you because you are different. Understand that David is ready to be king, and he has to learn the laws of leadership.

The Word called you out to a new place that today, many of us in the prophetic community have problems accepting because we want to hold on to where we were at. David has to learn the laws of his new position, which is not easy.

The prophet of today must understand that your biggest roadblock will be your focus on what has happened, how you were received, and your status within your prescribed circles of influence. Some laws govern the next level, and we need to know and understand the laws of prophetic leadership.

In other words, your vision of success is your roadblock as God takes you to another place. Prophets, we must learn the lesson of trying to hold on to a status versus moving to an unknown location in God by assignment and being successful in that assignment.

Do we trust God like that is the question? And do you know the laws of leadership in the prophetic realm?

CHAPTER 7

15 Laws of Prophetic Leadership

A law is a recognized principle whose violation must or should result in a penalty as failure, injury, loss, or pain. A prophetic law has binding rules that enforce and preside over a duty or obligation of a prophet.

The laws of prophetic leadership provide a description of a direct link between the cause and effect of a prophet's actions, obligations, and growth. Prophetic leadership has always seemed to rest and be tested on theory, spirituality, and social network norms.

If we want effective prophetic leadership, the bottom-line prophets must realize that we must practice what we will become. Learn how to become your prophet. Let us now look at some laws that David clearly learned along the way.

Much of today's prophetic movement is still in its infancy, as we continue to stress the need for prophetic education. Today, we have many theories based on differences in definitions and other basic characteristics. There are almost always formulated to fit a culture or a specific group.

So today, there is a great need for prophetic voices who will grow to become prophetic leaders. Prophetic leaders are individuals unbound by the worship of likability and committed to the integrity of the prophetic gift of God. These leaders search for themselves and their people and name the problems within as they grow in greatness.

While it does not mean we should be judgmental or harsh, it does mean we cannot serve God and people-please. If we, as the prophetic leaders of God, want to be known as the prophets of God, then we need the correction of prophetic voices who have matured and become prophetic leaders.

Even among prophetic leaders who will address the difficult topics, we see a focus on the prophets "out there," or the issues of the Body of Christ, rather than fixing the brokenness within our own prophetic ranks.

Do you ever notice those leaders who constantly rail against the world's sins but never turn their gaze to the dysfunctions of their inner circle or assigned prophets in training?

For those prophetic leaders who will tell you it takes much more boldness to call out the sins of their prophets and prophetic peers rather than it does to call out the sins of the culture.

Let me present 15 Prophetic Leadership Laws of the Prophet. You will see more about David and yourself here as I challenge you to find yourself. This will be your Cave of Adullam, especially for the emerging prophetic leaders.

Prophetic Law # 1.

As a prophetic leader, you must be about fulfilling your true destiny more than others expect of you. This is why you must master where you are before you move forth.

This was the young Jeremiah's and Jonah's issue; they both were worried about how they saw themselves rather than achieving the destiny God had for them.

Prophets your issues with people will cloud your decision-making process. Even today, we see this in Contemporary Prophets as they want the image, which they mistake for their destiny. Allow God to deal with you.

Prophetic Law # 2

Extraordinary Spirit ...Some Bible translations may call it a "spirit of excellence." Some versions refer to it as a "distinguished spirit." But in either case, the meaning remains the same. In David and Daniel's case, demeanor, disposition, and attitude were obvious attributes, clearly apparent to anyone. What was most evident was the spirit. The most obvious thing about the quality of an effective prophetic leader is their spirit. This is the spirit with which he serves.

This means not just a quality of his serving but the spirit with which he is teachable and learns. This is the spirit with which he speaks, not just the truth, but the leader can put words and phrases together to communicate a concept or idea. It is the spirit with which he prays.

It is the spirit with which the leader deals with people and relates to those around them. It is a spirit of excellence, a spirit that is extraordinary. It is a distinguishable spirit. That is one of the things that we must seek God to develop in us so that we become effective leaders with a spirit of excellence.

Prophetic Law # 3

As a prophet, you must realize you're a leader. We are leaders training leaders. This is our gift instinct; we know how to lead if we allow ourselves to learn how to follow. When that prophet ignores a prophet's leadership instinct, then the prophet becomes ineffective because the instincts of leadership are learning how to deal with those who follow.

Too many prophets never get the experience because they feel their secular job or profession qualifies them for instant prophetic leadership, and it does not.

The Prophet Balaam was not effective and indecisive as God's prophet because he was called to lead in a situation that tested him against his personal preferences.

He did not follow his basic instincts. He is called upon to lead in a difficult situation and does not know what to do. His instincts are off, and he does not realize the moment he is in.

Prophetic Leadership Law # 4

Prophetic leaders can't afford to grow stale. This usually happens when a prophet assumes the title of a prophet and never attempts to learn more of their gifting.

"Anything that we do for years that doesn't match the essence of your gift will eventually become monotonous and routine, ritualistic, and most of all frustrating." You then become a candidate to go back into the world.

One of Paul's inner circle students was a young man named Demas; he was pulled back into the world because he was unfilled. Paul, on the other hand, we see in *2 Timothy 4: 7-8* that his relationship with God never allowed his gifting to grow stale. He says, "I have kept the faith, fought the good fight, and finished my race." Prophetic leaders understand that you can't help people that do not want to be helped or will not go through the process.

Prophetic Leadership Law # 5

Knowledge and Insight: David was knowledgeable; he knew what to do. Proverbs says, "Do you see a man skilled in his work? He will not stand before obscure men. He will stand before kings."

Be skilled in who you are. God does not give medals for mediocrity. God wants you to develop your knowledge. Knowledge is understanding the facts and knowing the facts, and having the skills to go along with the facts. David developed himself on his way to becoming a great leader.

Prophetic Leadership Law # 6

Prophetic leaders, while your ministry is an excellent portion of your life. You must learn that you will need multiple skill sets for other areas of your life.

Understand that your gift will establish a relationship with God that will lead you in all life matters.

In other words, your gift is for the glory of God, not for your personal pleasure. Your gift puts you in a place to develop yourself. Ask David about that when you get to heaven.

Your gift can and will bring your personal pleasures. This does not mean you will be effective in moderating the pleasures without appearing to be greedy or "Insensitive." Again learn the lessons of David's life. Many people will always reflect on what they feel the prophet is or should be as they see it. You must develop a skill set for your business and personal lives.

Prophetic Leadership Law # 7

Prophetic leadership is not only when an individual can capably do what needs doing; Prophetic leadership is achieved when a person can implement what needs to be done through others. This was a specialty of David and Moses also.

This will be the foundation of your prophetic legacy. Who did you empower to be birthed in others that made a difference in someone else's life? David made a difference in the lives of countless others as a king and as a warrior. Moses birthed and empowered Joshua's life, who empowered the two spies who empowered Rahab *(Joshua Chapter 2)*.

Joseph indirectly influenced his brothers years later to repent and become better men as they learned from their mistakes with Joseph *(Genesis 45:4-7)*.

Prophetic Leadership Law # 8

Prophetic leaders with vision understand they must grow, and they understand that the vision they have can't be done just by them alone. When a prophetic leader operates independently, it stunts everybody's growth, including the leader.

When you are a prophetic leader, you must make every prophet aware that they matter to you and the overall operation of your goal.

If you don't or can't do this, you will grow people with the same independent spirit. Prophets, when you lead by the direction of God, you will embrace the fact that your vision is too big for only you to carry out; you need their help. To achieve your goals and directives, thus this creates avenues of opportunities for your subordinate prophets.

On social media platforms like Facebook, God gave me *The Prophets Teaching Group (TPTG)*. The Prophets Prayer line is another classic example of this; it allows prophets the opportunities to Horne their skills and become proficient in their gifts while it sustains the vision of Americans having a place to get prophetic ministry at almost any time. Prophetic leaders create a vision large enough that you cannot achieve it alone. Prophetic leaders must stop trying to be Islands.

Prophetic Leadership Law # 9

Prophetic leaders who are unfocused will never achieve. Prophetic leaders do not allow the criticisms of others or the distractions of questionable urgency to deter you from your destiny. Remember what your future is, and becoming distracted to keep the peace is becoming unfocused.

Which effectively removes you from your path of God's plan for your life, is not of God. Did David or Moses allow people to keep them from their time with God? The answer is no, even their harsh criticisms.

In *Numbers 14,* when everybody said Moses was a bad leader to his face, it was Moses who prayed for them to God, so God would not kill them when they vilified all people.

That's focus, and if you're going to lead prophets or anyone, you will run into this issue and deal with it until you solve it. We have outlined David's life and many of his obstacles, and we see how he handled his business.

Prophetic Leadership Law # 10.

Interpretation of Dreams: Daniel had an interpretation of dreams gifting. Can God speak through dreams? You bet He can. But does He exclusively speak through dreams? No! He speaks through the process of elements. He speaks through people. He speaks through double confirmations.

He speaks through anything that He can use to get to you. But what is the interpretation of dreams? Let me make this precise and succulent. It just means Daniel knew what God was saying.

He had an extraordinary spirit in times alone with His God, so he knew what God was saying. Prophets today seem to think it is a distraction to learn about dreams. They won't invest the time learning about the language of dreams but will make the investment so they can be recognized, just to be called a prophet and criticize other prophets who they don't know.

Prophetic Leadership Law # 11

Solve Difficult Problems: Daniel nor David ever saw a problem as a justification for dropping out or running away. Prophets never see a problem as a reason to "bail." You are going to have many problems that you are going to hit you in ministry and in leadership. Never see a problem as a justification for mediocrity or to bail out.

One of the qualities of an effective prophetic leader is that they can solve complex problems. God will never send you into battle if you cannot stand up in the barracks.

There are going to be complex problems. Always see them as a step toward effective leadership. Difficulties challenged David as they did Daniel also. God is always available. That will help you to move from phase to phase as you develop into an effective leader.

Prophetic Leadership Law # 12

Prophetic Leaders are coachable. They have been in the trenches; they tend to rise through the ranks and see the organization from various angles and positions.

When leaders understand they will always crawl before walking, they will offer a broad and diverse experience for people and prophets who have failed and want to learn something from what went wrong. People and prophets who shrugged it off and kept going kept making the same mistakes over and over. Prophetic leaders are in the Fox hole leaders.

This type of prophet is not disillusioned with unrealistic expectations as Elijah did after Mt. Carmel *(1 King 18-19)*. There will always be unexpected and demonic overtures throughout life. Elijah only recovered because he had been in the trenches with God.

Prophetic Leadership Law # 13

Prophetic leaders find a place in their lives that stinks. They then work and work to achieve success in that place. If the stench of failure drives you, then you are well on your way to learning how to grow into a leader that will be effective for God.

Great leaders are not pushed; they are driven to abandon something they detest. Let go and tenacity will come from the places that stink in our lives to achieve victory.

Prophetic Leadership Law # 14

Prophetic leaders must learn that pursuing their passion is proof of their calling. Many apostles, seers, and prophets struggle to identify their passion and gifting. Your purpose is in your passions, not just what you love but passionately hate.

When you discover where you make a difference at them, you will find the essence of your gift, and it will renew itself to you constantly, which will be reflected in your passion for what you do. Say you're called to healing but don't know it. Your focus and passion will turn you to healing. You will sense the need to learn as much as possible and trust God to develop the gift. Scripture says in *Hebrews 11* that God is a rewarder of them who will diligently seek Him. Prophetic leaders, what are you seeking?

Prophetic Leadership Law # 15

Dealing with enigmas, an enigma is an unexplainable item that is hard to explain. It is just tough to understand. David and Daniel come to mind here. Both were able to take difficult concepts and make them simple. This is a relationship issue with God. Prophetic leaders, soak this up.

Now that we have looked at David and other prophets of God, we now have a good idea about leadership. I would encourage you to still study this chapter because you will have to know what voice to follow in your life.

So many of us will say, "I follow God," and we will go out of our way to prove we follow God, and in reality, our life and conduct are virtually the total opposite. I need to share this because there is a voice that we can refer to as voice number four. Voice number four is a voice that we so often believe is God, and it is not. The reality is it is not the devil either. Let's meet voice number four. It is a voice that David conquered in his life, and prophet you will also.

CHAPTER 8

The Issues Of Voice Number Four In A Prophet's Life.

What voice are you living with and responding to? There are voices we all hear as prophets. These voices are real, yet they guide our lives as we go forth.

Depending on the voice you live with and respond to, your progress will be stopped, or your progress will be sporadic or expedient. Here I want you to focus on David and see how he handled this voice. Let's go back and reread the previous chapters, especially chapter 1, and come back if you need to. This may be critical in your understanding of visualization and how the prophet actually saw in Adullam.

Prophets are leaders, but leaders are stable in crisis and consistent in times of inconsistency. The prophetic leader will speak as commanded because the voice of relevance will always be the voice the prophet chooses to listen to. Let me explain more.

A man may, but God will not call you to what you can't manifest without his help. This is why the voice you respond to will be the voice that will make or break you. So what happens when the prophet listens to a voice that they can't escape, and that voice is the voice that is destroying the prophet's life? I want to examine the agents of influence a prophet will listen to.

There are four voices that a prophet will listen to, but voice number four is the key voice that will destroy us. Voice number four is a voice that has and can continue to destroy groups of emerging prophets of God.

Voice number four will stop your life in its tracks. Voice number four will hinder and erase your progress. Voice number four is so important to your quality of life that many of us may not realize it.

Voice number four is a voice that, unless dealt with, will destroy your ministry, family, and life. Let's identify voice number 4, but before we do, let's look at voices 1-3, so we understand voice number four better.

Voice number one is the voice of God. God speaks to us in our spirits, communicating His will through our souls. Most of us, as prophets, spend most of our thought life in our heads. *Romans 8:7* speaks of "the mind of the flesh."

Because of this, our soul is focused on the sensory world around us. Our physical senses, thoughts, desires, and emotions are constantly being bombarded and stimulated in worldly, carnal, and fleshly ways.

Voice number two" is the voice of the devil. The devil has crafty ways of speaking to us, which he has perfected. He is subtle. He throws thoughts into our minds like flaming arrows and tells us through the worldly ideas and viewpoints that he has injected into other people. Prophets, *Ephesians 6:16* tells us that we must "extinguish all the flaming arrows of the evil one."

Voice number three is the voice of other people. Sometimes people say things that are true, noble, and good, and sometimes people say things that are just the opposite. What are you hearing from the "voice" of other people? We see many now-generation prophets swayed by the voice of other people.

1 King 19 shows us that God will put a voice in your life just as he did Elisha. Elisha listened to Elijah, and we saw how he turned out. What is unfortunate is that pride and arrogance stop us, as prophets, and leads us to depend on the fatal version of voice number four.

Voice number four is the voice of the prophet. It is your voice, and we all must be very concerned with what we are saying to ourselves.

All the voices are important, but voice number four is the voice that is perhaps the most obvious because it is our own voice. Voice number four is our speaking voice, the voice of our soul.

This is the voice we talk to ourselves with. This is the voice inside our heads? How many of us see images and pictures inside our heads because our voice is running wild? Imagine your voice telling you that you will never be this or that. Can you imagine if David only listened to himself?

This is the voice; it is your voice saying that you will never attain a certain status in God. Your voice tells you that you will never be anointed to do this or do that. Your voice tells you that you are a failure, second class, or never will be relevant in your ministry.

We all have emotions, feelings, and desires because of our voice. We will refer to the voice as voice number four; it is our personal voice and our self-conversation voice, as we speak to ourselves. Voice number four can talk us into, or it can talk us out of something.

Look closely, and the soul is at work here. Our minds tell us what we think. Our will tells us what we want and our emotions tell us how we feel. The Bible refers to our minds, will, and emotions as our "flesh nature." When our soul is not subjected to God, we are listening to our flesh nature. The soul is the human computer, and it has to be programmed for a prophet with God's Word.

How many of us are willing to admit that voice number four has affected our walk with God? Prophet, this is the one voice you must know, and not allow it to rule or destroy you. Have you ever considered how many prophets of God are in mental institutions because they listened to the wrong version of voice number four?

As Prophets, we tend to live on the shallow surface, so to speak; we rarely venture deeper where the Spirit of God lives within us. The reason is that our soul has not connected with our spirit.

How many have the prophetic gift and do not know how to hear and be led by our spirits? Do we understand that we leave ourselves open to the devil's deception? Fear or the thought of a troublesome situation that you have come out of, and you hear your voice telling you that there is a chance that you will go back.

The enemy will always use a thought or an experience that he will use to put you in the mentality of failure. You may have come out of a storm, and you find yourself listening to your voice about going back to that. This is voice number four; it is dangerous and destructive if it is allowed to run wild.

Prophet, God's blessing can be upon your life, yet voice number four speaks to you and ruins the status you have labored for so long to attain. This voice is haunting and defiant, and it will nag you. Can you imagine that this voice will not allow you to relax, especially with the call of the prophet, seer, watchman, or apostle upon your life?

Voice number four can take your life to a level of self-destruction that is basically uncontrollable. The work of voice number four is to feed your faith, or it will feed your fear. There is a reality that the prophet of God must stop talking to themself in a destructive manner.

This is why we develop, and then we simply stop. We feel we can't go higher in God; we feel lost or in a place where God does not want us to be, and we stop ascending. We are listening to voice number four. Voice number four will keep the prophet in a holding pattern all their life.

Think about this, we have ascended to a position to do an assignment for God, and we have stopped growing. We are satisfied being leaders, but our ability to impart has ceased.

We were called to impart and raise, yet voice number four tells us we are tired and there is no need. God has said to continue, but we did not because we were listening to voice number four and positioning ourselves for trouble.

Moses could tell us plenty on voice number four. Remember when he was so upset that he spoke to the children of Israel as heathens and disobeyed God? The great Moses listens to voice number four, and God removes him from his assignment. This is serious and critical.

Voice number four has a vital part in how we are healed and how we live our lives. There is the woman with the issue of blood. She used voice number four, which was the voice that healed her.

Her ability to use voice number four demonstrates how vital this voice is. This voice is voice number four to manifest what we need and want in life. She speaks to herself constantly, "If I could touch the hem of his garment."

Over and over again, she speaks that to herself; she convinces herself that if she can touch the garment of Jesus. All she wanted and needed to do was have a touch, and she knew she would be made whole. Have you considered that there was absolutely no scripture to back her voice up?

Her voice in her head was speaking life and faith to her situation. Have you ever considered that she did not have the permission of Jesus to touch Him? This woman did not talk with the disciples before; she pushed her way to Jesus to touch Him.

She acted after listening to voice number four, and now it was a part of her; it was her point of contact to connect with that which was holy. This is how powerful voice number four is in our lives.

Prophet, what are you telling yourself? What are you saying to yourself about where you are right now? How many of us speak debt-free, wealth, prosperity, healing, and deliverance in our lives? The principle works if we only perform the principle in our lives, prophets.

The voices in your life that tell you what you can't do and what you are not are the voices that destroy the promises of God in your life. What version of voice number four are you listening to, and how is it affecting your life?

The prophet must realize that it will take word to combat it. This is how we deal with the demonic version of voice number four. Look at the fact that when the prophet does not have a strong foundation of God's Word in their life, there is a place for voice number four to destroy them.

How do you not speak life to yourself prophet? Consider that we are expected to speak life to others, and yet we very well may be talking death to ourselves. Every prophet will have a voice of negativity in their life. Your voice number four will be dealt with by flooding your life with God's Word.

Prophet, unless you speak to those harmful voices, the enemy will not be shut down in your life. The ability to function in the realm of God will be hindered.

Notice that Jeremiah had issues with this, and Moses had problems with this. They are two prime examples of prophets who demonstrate listening to opposing voices and having to make changes within themselves.

Prophet, whatever negative voice in your life that you will not shut down will hinder your development as a prophet. Could it be the voice of others who tell you certain things about yourself that dispute what God is telling you?

You may be affected by voice number four as you try to learn who you are. Your voice tells you everything you can't do, and God tells you that you can do everything.

This is why the most challenging assignments go to God's prophets, and He trusts us. Let's explore this with visualization in more depth as seeing God send you to a place where there is no life, and He expects you to produce.

Prophet, what voice will you choose to believe? Over and over again, we see the prophet must listen to God. We must listen despite what we see or feel. This is where David was a specialist. Can you imagine being chosen to minister to the dead?

These are the types of assignments that God sends specialist prophets to. Now let's see prophet if you can find your vision in this type of situation. Yes, God did send a prophet to minister among the dead.

CHAPTER 9

A Prophet Chosen To Minister To The Dead

When you take your first breath, your beliefs begin to shape your perceptions consciously of your environment. Would you consider that limiting beliefs come through your parents, siblings, and surroundings?

This should help you understand the Illegitimate Bastard Curse of the Prophet, which we addressed in Chapter Two. Yes, it is important to understand that and see why.

To appreciate the genius of David, you have to understand his prophetic faith and the level it developed to. This chapter will address the level of David's faith in the form of another prophet named Ezekiel, but I will also reflect upon us and where we have to go.

Our beliefs are shaped and formed into the landscape of our personal realities. Your reality as a prophet is a result that affects your imagination and behavior. You are tested as you go and never forget that.

Consider seeing something thousands of years before it happens. Imagine that and imagine the prophetic word you speak as it rings in the atmosphere for thousands of years, and it is that word that changes people's lives. Let's look at this.

1948 was a year of fulfillment for the Jews. Many of you, like me, were not born in 1948, but those who suffered the atrocities of the Jewish people really would remember the hard days leading up to 1948. These were some tough times for the Jewish people.

The Jews are a people like the African Americans and Native Americans, who have been dehumanized over many years of their lives. The term dehumanized is a term to represent the attitude towards a race of people in which one thinks it is better than the other. To degrade is to destroy systemically.

Stories, tales, rumors, slang terms, and actions of humiliation and directed violence will tear people down and eventually stir hate enough to kill and destroy a race or a culture of people.

When we use the term dehumanize, it is a process to lower the person, the platform, or the status of the destroyed ones. This was the case with the Native Americans, African Americans, and Jewish people.

From 1933-1945, the name Adolph Hitler, the German leader, rang drama and crisis for the Jewish people. Under his watch, they are hurt, disrespected, killed, and families separated, all because of hate.

Hitler felt the Jewish people were not important as compared to the German people. This is how he justified his systematic racism. Genocide has now happened, and the horror the Jewish people suffered is beyond words.

In 1948 we saw the Jews come together as Israel again became a nation, all this after at least 6 million of them were destroyed. Many biblical historians support that *Ezekiel 37* is the prophecy of 1948 as the people come back together. Can you prophet, visualize this? This is important for you to see and understand how it relates to David, being able to see in Adullam.

Ezekiel 37 is a chapter that deals with death, pain, and the real-life struggle of people. A real-life struggle that God shows His prophet concerning the Jewish people. The lesson we learned from the Jewish people is that we can and will survive despite the struggle. We will come back because it is the will of God.

The lesson we learn about the prophet is that God will use us for the most challenging assignments, even to a graveyard of death to prophesy it. Visualize this, for David, Adullam was his valley of death, where he learned how to see.

Ezekiel 37 is a struggle of a people that is so real that the outcome is a valley of death. They have been destroyed. Can you imagine standing in a valley so full of dry bones that the only sound you hear is your personal movement? This is an example of a prophet being put by God in a situation and the personal struggle to obey God in a life-defining assignment.

Ezekiel is a seer. His gift is an extraordinary visionary revelation as God spoke to him through visions. He is a prophet who saw revelation through symbolism. Please understand and accept the fact his gift was at a level that many seek today.

His work we see in scripture is unique, to say the least. The fact that Ezekiel speaks to us through his experience of his visions is such a powerful tool to understand how God will use a prophet in a situation that stretches Ezekiel to his very core.

Let's look at *Ezekiel 37:1-12*. Ezekiel speaks about being placed in the midst of the valley of the dry bones. He is looking around and taking account of the bones, and there is an incredible number. He describes the bones as being brittle and, of course, dry.

God speaks to him and asks him a simple question that is already known. God says, "Can these dry, brittle bones live?" This is a test of faith that must be passed. Ezekiel is told to prophesy upon these bones. God speaks to him to address the bones to hear the Word of God.

The obedience of Ezekiel sparks God to say that the breath of life will come into what was dead and lifeless. The awesome Word of God spoke life into what was not. Ezekiel demonstrates a gift that few like David had.

He speaks, and as Ezekiel speaks, life comes and shows itself. Notice how he describes the bones as they come together with the muscles and tendons. Then he witnesses the skin, and to see the process and power of God's Word is incredible.

I often wonder if any of us, the now-generation prophets, could deal with this and not want to run. The asking is a fair question to ask if we will be honest with ourselves.

Ezekiel reaches a new level, and yet he is not there. Does this remind you of an elevated David who needs to go to another level to fulfill his God-given assignment?

The bones were now figures, but they were lifeless. One thing to consider is that we cannot assume anything from God. Our trust in God is put to the test. Ezekiel is tested when God tells him to prophesy unto the winds.

We see his faith tested as he speaks to the four winds, and life comes into the figures. God has shown His prophet life in an environment that he can understand and yet stretched him. Can you visualize this and can you see this in your life?

Ezekiel was in the valley of the dry bones and his ability to practice visualization and see the plan of God has taken him to another level in his prophetic mantle. The prophet's obedience here is seen, and it is noted that God is now ready to reveal even more to him.

God tells Ezekiel that this is the house of Israel. The gifts of the great Prophet Ezekiel are clearly on display. God is a restorer and wants to restore His people, and we have to understand that His servants will have to stand and deal with the atrocities of the world that we are presented with.

This is a key reason why things happen the way they do in our lives. Consider your life and your assignment, and now let's look at what we experienced and see how it fits and prepared you for now.

Ezekiel demonstrates the qualities of David as his visionary gifts are on full display, and his ability to obey God in the face of total death. This is so important prophet.

Ezekiel is a prophet of extreme epic proportions, and his work is second to none. He describes a situation he has been placed in that is death personified. God has put him in a place of death. This is a spiritually dry place.

This is a place where God will send His prophets to minister. Have you ever been to a place where they see you coming, start cussing, or start demonic chatting? Ezekiel has been sent to a place that is so dry he constantly describes the bones as being very dry; a place of death where the prophet is more obedient than he believes.

God has taken him to a place he has never seen before, and he could not imagine, and his belief is stretched. If you're afraid that God will stretch you, you limit your usefulness to God. The most stressful situation you may be in is the situation that will develop you the most.

The valley of dry bones represents a valley of a defeated army within the House of Israel. This is why we see and know it is Israel and the Jewish people who have been scattered all over the earth.

God is showing His prophet this vision, a prophetic picture of Israel, and how He will reconnect His people, despite the struggle. Every ethnic race should read this and understand this.

What's important is to realize there will be a day of reckoning for all who have experienced racism on an institutional level. This is why you, as a prophet, a seer, and an apostle, are called, and when you consider it as useless as you may feel with this pandemic and social issues, you must realize that this is your time.

Ezekiel is challenged to minister amid death. He is not comfortable. This is like God sending you to the local undertaker, and God says, "Prophesy to everything in here that is dead." The reality of being in such a situation now becomes real beyond words for Ezekiel, and we reflect on his personal growth as a prophet.

Here he is in the midst of a valley of total dry bones, total death, and no life, and God is asking him, in the midst of death, can something live, namely the bones? We must consider Ezekiel and his mindset.

He knows God has placed him somewhere for a specific reason. God will put you in a situation to develop you, and no matter how much you know or what you have seen, there is still more of God that He constantly reveals.

God has warned Ezekiel what will happen thousands of years before it does. Can you handle information of this kind? A better question is can God trust you with information thousands of years before it happens? The Word of God to His prophet then and now is an unchangeable reality.

Where are the Issachar seers who God has shown what awaits us in the next season? Where are the Issachar seers speaking to the leaders of nations, saying thus said the Lord?

Prophet, it is no accident that many of us are like Ezekiel, and we may have faith, yet we get put in a situation and tell God,

"Oh Lord, thou knoweth." God asks us, His prophets, seers, and apostles, can my people be trusted with trouble?

Can my people deal with Coronavirus? Can my people deal with asthenic racism and rise from it? Can the Native Americans ever be restored? Can African Americans ever achieve equality? Listen as the prophet says, "Oh Lord, you know, but as you command, I will speak, I will prophesy as you command."

Today for some Jewish people, this is the worst situation. They recall the issues of parents or grandparents, and although uncomfortable, the reality is that God sent a prophet who would obey and call into existence what He had promised in His Word.

A word was spoken thousands of years before an actual event, and we see God again prove His Word. Question? Can God send you? Who has God shown a situation because God has uniquely chosen you to see the next season?

Ezekiel is proven trustworthy. He knows he is at his limit among death on top of death and now he is called to prophesy to what he knows is dead, and he obeys God. Prophet, do you really want to see these types of things in your life? Do you have the capacity to handle this type of drama?

Imagine, as a prophet, you are the element of change, and you are seeing something that you're not sure about, but you know that God can change it if He wants to. The bones had been dry for so long until the reality before the prophet is concerning because the prophet sees the decay of an army defeated, a group of men and women who are dehumanized, and the only thing left is their bones, and that is rapidly growing up.

God takes His prophet on a trip that challenges the prophet's intellect. Ezekiel did not believe in the mission, but he obeyed God's assigned work. Welcome to developing as a prophet, where your obedience is better than a sacrifice.

You are in the middle of a dead city, a quiet town, a dead state, or even a dead nation. God is speaking to you to prophesy to the dead bones; speak to them and see God use them mighty.

This issue is whether you can handle the stress and pressure of your deadly situation. Have you noticed that God has a special place where He blesses His prophet? Ezekiel is blessed in all places, in the valley of the dry bones.

How about you? I want to explore this as we look for that special place. Remember, we also pointed out that Adullam was not the place David chose to go and be blessed. It was the place God led him to bless him.

Bottom line prophet, the Word of God, is the first step to taking action on what needs to happen in any situation. We now again look closer at David and understand his situation in the cave at Adullam. There are special places that God will use to bless His prophets. Let's learn even more about visualization and David as he sees in Adullam.

CHAPTER 10

God's Special Place for The Prophet's Blessings

Faith is a gift from God. As prophets, our faith in God is very important to our everyday life. When we operate in works by faith, we work by mental exertion instead of physical force. God gives our words as God works by our faith."

David is in the cave of Adullam, operating on the very fuel of his faith. He is there and believes God will sustain him as he is at his wit's end. Look closely again at this. We will see examples of David's mentality here, but we will also see ours.

As prophets, we can see that there is a faith that God operates and rules in the heavens and sustains us in life's challenges. It enables us to endure without yielding and bear the trials of our time and era. This faith has characterized the lives of prophets throughout history.

The prophet must understand that we must see and know a faith that is able to move mountains. We can no longer keep limiting God by our faith in Him. Without faith in God's servants, there will be suffering and no miracles. Our jobs as prophets are too big and too essential to God's plan for humanity.

This is important because God has always sent us His prophets to "restore" knowledge of the gospel back to the earth. We, the prophets, must walk in an extraordinary level of faith.

In *Amos 8:11-12*, the prophet Amos said, "People will stagger from sea to sea." He added that they would wander from north to east. He followed that up by saying, "They will search for the Word of the Lord, but they will not find it."

The reality is that you could search the entire earth for the gospel of God, and no matter how hard you search, if there is no prophet or even one willing to stand in the gap prophetically on the earth, you won't find it. In *Amos 3:7*, no one ever just "figured out" the will of God, His plans or secrets, without it being revealed to them first through prophets.

This brings up an undeniable basic fact. You cannot accept Christ without first accepting His prophets. This is what intrigues me about David. David was gifted in many ways, and he knew who he was. Prophet, you must be the same.

Prophet, this is why you must know who you are. There can be no doubt in your knowing who you are. Your faith will keep you connected to God so that you can complete your assignment. Can you see how David demonstrated this?

Prophets know this. We would have no clue who Christ is without the teachings of the prophets. It would be crazy to say that we accept and believe in Christ while simultaneously rejecting the witness of John the Baptist, His prophet then, and you and I, His prophets now.

When Jesus speaks to the scribes and Pharisees about accepting dead prophets and rejecting living prophets, He speaks of the prophets that'll be sent in the future. *Matthew 23:39 says, "We will not see him henceforth."*

This will not happen until we say, "Blessed is he, that will come in the name of the Lord." How can we say we know God and speak death and disbelief to his prophets? This echoes a theme among growing prophets that they must be sure of the calling because of how people may or may not receive them. David has demonstrated this over and over.

Matthew 23:37 makes this sound like us in the now day world. "O Jerusalem, you have killed the prophets. You dared to stone them which are sent unto thee." This pattern of God sending prophets to His children has been going on for thousands of years. It started with Abraham, Moses, and others. They were rejected. Prophets were sent to people who must know and understand that they may be left. Their faith must be in God.

So the prophet, what happens when everything in your world drains your faith and you can't find relief? You find yourself in a situation that looks like all is lost, and yes, you know they keep telling you that prophet, if faith without works, is dead; likewise, works without faith are dead.

You're at the point of losing faith, and there is no reference point in your life that you feel you can claim and act on your faint. This was David in the Cave of Adullam.

There are some things and facts we must understand and accept. Prophets, with our faith, things can happen. A prophet, by exercising their faith, can cause things to happen. *Matthew 9:29 says, "According to your faith be it unto you."*

Prophet, so now, when nothing is working in your life, *Luke 5:4-7* tells us a story that we know so well. Jesus tells Simon to launch out into the deep. The story is that Simon has fished all night with other fishermen, and there is no catch.

Jesus uses their boat to speak to the people; never in their wildest dreams did they see the blessing coming. Many times, like the fisherman, they are frustrated and irritated, and here they are washing their nets, and Jesus says, "Launch your nets out." Launch them out into the deep.

Learn this right now, as a prophet, your gift is not in the shadow areas of life but develops and prospered in the deep areas of life. We must launch out in the deep, just like the fish. David went to his enemy; this was his deep as he developed his gifts.

We must learn from this that it is not time to give up, even when you have used all your resources. Blessings are waiting for us beyond our ability to imagine. How many prophets have lost precious time in their lives because they gave up? They were unwilling to go into the deep.

Now we see that things are not going well; people are talking and speaking doubt and disbelief towards and about you. Friends are walking away and acting funny, and you are now stuck with a decision to move forth, or you can give up. This is your chance to move in that David kind of faith, where you are not moved by what you see, but by what you believe.

Picture this, your resources are gone, your faith is lacking, and everything you have is on the line, and now you see nothing but the situation, and God says, "Launch out again," but this launch is out in the deep.

You must go out, and there is no assurance of a reference point in your mind, in your logic to justify the Word of God. "This is the place God has for me," you say to yourself.

You can't give up. You will never receive the blessing when you promised God you would go all the way, and your word does not come in agreement with His Word. Look closer, the nets are in a shadow place, but Jesus is telling them to launch out to a place they believe they have already been.

Remember, prophet, what do you do when you believe you have already done and given your best? Yet you know that God is saying there is more to you, and God is saying go deeper. David did it, and it worked for him, and it will work for you.

The lesson we learn here is that God is not a shadow. Your gift is not in the shadow areas. The blessings to enhance your gift are in the deep. God is the God of a new thing, and we are being sent out to a place where He instructs us to. This is about understanding who is who and not relying on us, prophets. This is about us relying on God.

The reality is that nothing worked for the fisherman, all night and nothing, and now they are being told to launch out into the very deep. Faith will take you places you have never been, and it will take you out of your comfort zone. Let's look at David yet again. Faith will take you places you have never been.

Did they believe in the Word enough to go deeper? Do we, as prophets, believe in the Word enough to go deeper? They did, and they found their blessing. Simon said, "At thy word."

Can you trust that Word without a referred point? You feel you need a justification, and God wants your obedience. Note here that your obedience directly results from your relationship with God.

The reality is that God will only bless in "the deep," as we see here. Notice that the fisherman was blessed at the level of their investment, and since God is no respecter of a person, we are affected by this. The issue here is that when the nets were dropped in the deep, things changed on the Word of the Lord.

A fisherman knows the waters he fishes in. He knows his craft. These fishermen had to fight through everything they knew to be true and logical to follow "the Word." God now knows that they are ready to be blessed. Simon never says nevertheless, "At your Word, we will launch again, this time out in the deep."

The question is, are you willing to obey to experience the blessing God has for you? Prophet, what do you expect when you pray to God to bless you? What do you expect when you pray to God for a financial blessing and God says to give what you have?

Too many prophets believe that we will wake up one morning and the illness will be gone or that a financial breakthrough will occur. Unfortunately, we have seen that life doesn't work that way. Prophets, we must understand that God has a way. He alone has a way for us to win.

God has created spiritual laws that we should abide by. One of the foremost spiritual laws is belief anchored by our faith in God. Can you believe what you say when we pray and do not doubt in our hearts, then we shall have what we pray for?

This is not debatable. We must believe. If you need a financial blessing, believe as you connect it to God with your faith, and do the same if you need healing in your body. Prophets must be like the fishermen when we are at our wit's ends dealing with a situation.

Mark 11:22-24 tells us to have faith in God. God says we should accept it and believe. We are not to doubt that God's will is going to be done. When we pray, we are to believe that we will receive.

In *Mark 11:12-14,* Jesus said to have faith in God. Jesus then says they could do what is physically impossible (or seemingly so) if they believe what they say in their hearts. Therefore, when we are at our lowest, it is our faith in God when we want to quit and our faith when we want to give up. Somehow I just never did see David giving up. I could see him getting frustrated but I could not see him giving up. How about you?

As a prophet of God, are you willing to do what God gives you to do? Do you or will you carry out the will of God? Are you willing to do what you must to experience God's blessings? Yes, you are already blessed but make no mistake, God has greater for you.

Our development is contingent on the opportunities to practice patience and develop it in our lives as we deal with life's problems. We learned in *Luke 5* that God is not a shadow God. When you ask God to improve your marriage, ministry, and life, many prophets expect you to wake up the next day and everything will be fresh, new, and beautiful.

You will probably be sadly mistaken. Instead, you will find that you will have to improve your marriage, ministry, and life not on the surface, but in the deep places. We want the promised blessings, and they are in the deep. We have to go out to get them; they are in the deep, not in the shadow.

Are you the prophet who wants a financial breakthrough and God says, "Yes? Now go to the School of the Prophet. Sow $_____$ at the school." You don't see it now because you're looking at the surface of the situation, but your seed launches you into the deep. The blessings were in the deep, the sacrifice through your obedience. Don't you see? The financial breakthrough is yours; it has already been promised through the Word of God.

God has your blessing in the deep, and you must move to the position of being in line to be blessed.

The fisherman obeyed, but they only did follow because they believed. This is a function that takes place in the heart, not just the head. Prophet, you may intellectually accept something but not believe it as if you believed something you see every day. That's a clear, simple fact.

We need to get our hearts to believe the Word of God. Let me now transfer your mind to fully understand going in the deep. Here we go. We need to transform our minds so that we think according to what the Word of God tells us instead of what worldly experiences tell us.

The Word of God has to be greater than natural experiences. We want to reach the point where our natural experiences are supernatural because God is directly involved in our lives through His Word and our obedience to it. This is where we want to be. This is the deep.

Visualization is a great tool to prepare the prophet to see this reality. Notice David saw himself fully in Adullam and you will experience this also in your special place. Who is ready to launch out into the deep?

Who is ready to see what God has for you in the deep? Who is ready to trust God in the place of the unseen, unheard, and unimagined? This is the place God wants to bless you. This is where the windows of heaven will be opened, and blessings will be poured out where there is no room to receive them.

God will not bless us in the shadow waters; He will bless us in the deep places. The places He has hidden for us, His prophets. Jesus said for us first to have faith in God. This means that we are leaning on God and putting our confidence in God for whatever it is we believe.

However, that faith would be meaningless if God has not already provided whatever we accept Him for. True faith is to look at the Word of God and see what it reveals to us about God's provision and grace, and then we believe it and expect it to happen just as the Word reveals.

A prophet not only prophesies of things that will happen, but we, the prophets, have come in these last days to testify of Jesus Christ and to lay down any contention over who He is. Over 1500 years of confusion and darkness have existed, and the remnants of the living prophets have revealed and restored a true knowledge of the Lord Jesus Christ.

Without prophets, we'd be left to philosophical speculations about God. While that will rub some theologians the wrong way, the fact of *Ephesians 2:20* is not to be disputed. The church is built on the gifts of the apostle and the prophet, with Jesus Christ as the Chief cornerstone.

Psalm 1:1-3 reveals David's inner thoughts; let's examine his reflections. He speaks that the man who knows where he walks at is blessed. This type of man or woman knows who is who in their lives. The ability to know that God is your provider and your consoler in times of stress is what we need to delight ourselves in God. David reveals so much of himself as he speaks that he shall be like a tree planted that is blessed and will bring forth prosperity in due season. David said, "Whatever he does shall prosper." God will prosper the things that you do.

This is life in general. This happens because one delights in the Word of God and meditates on it consistently. God will prosper the things that you do. We should be doing something. We already should know that we have to seek God and His ways and, of course, trust Him.

David's mantle is a metaphor for *Matthew 6:33*. Seek the kingdom of God, and the blessings of God will follow. Prophet, seek God as you venture out into the deep! Our relationship with the Lord is the number one priority. Seek the Lord with your whole heart, and you will be blessed. This blessing may not look like what you might expect, but it is there nonetheless.

Do you remember that David still found a blessing in his worst of times, even after being king? Consider that Solomon was born after David's biggest personal defeat. That was a blessing for David even after he had sinned.

We seek the Lord, and then we live according to His ways. *James 1:22* tells us that we must be doers of God's Word. Most of the time, our lip service allows us to simply hear each other. This is so childlike. This was a critical mistake in David's life, and I must explore it. This will affect us.

The reality is that we have mortgaged our destiny because we act like children. We are like children many times in the prophetic. We are masters of deceiving ourselves. Employing visualization in this may be harder for some of you than others, but we must get there.

I want to discuss this as we look at the apostles and prophets and why we tend to be kid-like. We do not seem to be in the process of reaching our destiny; that seems clear, especially when we need to go out into the deep! David's deep was in the Cave of Adullam. Let you and I find ours.

CHAPTER 11

Apostles And Prophets Understanding The Mentality Of Your Personal Destiny

Have you ever felt that you may have been a barrier or a block to your destiny? The apostle and the prophet are the foundation gifts of the church, with Jesus as the Chief Cornerstone. According to Ephesians 2:20, the church's cornerstone gifts are often scrutinized and most attacked.

How many groups of believers do we see who are intent on not including these five gifts of the 5-fold ministry within their fellowship? Some would instead block out the apostle and the prophet for various reasons. This is how some people felt about David.

Consider that prophets have hurt some people; some have yet to be educated in the 5-fold ministry concept of Ephesians chapter four. Then some simply do not believe in the concept of a 5-fold ministry.

All that is true, and it continues to be an issue, but what about the apostle and the prophet, who need to understand but do not understand their personal process of destiny? So why are we still reflecting on David here? You will see it shortly.

Over and over, we see this apostle or prophet, and they are in love with tomorrow and not today. They are in love with who they want to be tomorrow, and they fail to address the issues of their lives today. Did you notice that David became in love with his authority when he should have been fighting with his troops? He is looking at another man's wife. He had to fail before he succeeded.

Today for the apostle and prophet is important because, without today, tomorrow does not matter. Reaching your destiny is learning how to master your current step on the way to your next step in life. This is what you have to admire about David. This is why he is an example to prophets and apostles.

Today we see the prophets and the apostle searching for validation, place to place in the Body of Christ, and they never seem to grow. They do not realize that they could be their most significant obstacle to fulfilling their God-given destiny in the struggle to understand and grow.

Notice that David realized this as he spent seven days fasting and interceding for his child with Uriah's wife. He knew he had to get before God. He knew he was wrong; he also knew what God had spoken to him through the prophet Nathan. David dealt with this upfront. You must give him credit for that.

What holds a prophet or apostle back from building fruitful and anointed relationships? Have you ever wondered? What is the issue of life that has these anointed servants of God in a place of stalemate? The issue happens far too often, and we must look into the Word of God to find an issue.

Turn your attention to *1 Corinthians 13:11*. When I was a child, the Word of God says that I thought, talked, and acted as a child. This is what happened to David. He was thinking like a child. He had everything, but like a child wanted what he saw and knew it was not his. His ability to be in leadership and function as a child hurt everyone. This is what happens today.

When I became a man/woman, the Word says that childish things were put away. This is important because we look at the world in a certain way. Look closely at *1 Corinthians 13:11* again.

There are two different communication systems. The two systems need to be addressed in the life of the work of the apostle or prophet. There is the system of the child or immature mentality, and there is the system of being a mature adult.

We need to examine each to understand the effect each. This will impact the life of an apostle or prophet as far as development. This is directly affected by the view of how we see our destiny. The destiny of an apostle or prophet will only be understood or reached once they change their communication from a child to an adult.

Thinking, speaking, and understanding as a child differs from thinking, speaking, and understanding as an adult. Let's look at how we look at others and how we look at ourselves. We will always test others by how they think, speak, and what they do or do not understand.

As apostles and prophets, when we look at our ministry work, do we have the courage to test ourselves? Could we operate as kids or children when our position requires us to operate as adults? What are we communicating or holding on to that limits our assignments and clouds our destiny?

This is the key to understanding our destiny. Do we function at the level we need to, and more importantly, are we aware we must test ourselves? This is a far question; we need to ask ourselves! Look again at how David handled himself, even in his drama. Read *2 Samuel 11-12* for the detailed story.

How many of us know and understand that many of us with prophetic and apostolic gifts are loyal to our dysfunctions? How many of us in the apostolic or prophetic will be stubborn and hold on to ways that clearly are not working?

We claim that growth is not leading you to your destiny because you may be thinking, acting, or even communicating as a child. How many of us have heard phrases such as "that's how I am or speak for yourself?" We all have heard, "This is the way God told me to do it."

Why do we not consider that the way we say is not working? A better question is, how much longer will so many of us hold on to our dysfunctions and allow life to pass us by?

We are doing things as a child in an environment that we need to do as adults. We are hurting ourselves. Today we see the differences between prophets and apostles even within their ranks. The childish ways have separated us greatly within the ranks of the apostolic and prophetic. The core issue that separates them is how they communicate.

This is how they speak, think, and act. Can you see that the way you think, speak, or act is your announcement of your maturity or you being immature or childish? This is the link to your destiny.

It is hard to understand that God is putting you in positions of influence and because of how you see them and how you feel about them, you do not understand your journey to your destiny.

This is critical to the prophet and apostle as they relate to the Body of Christ. The real issue is the inability to understand a need for change in an apostle or prophet. This is the status of the inner man.

What am I saying? The outer life of the apostle and the prophet are seen, and they are fine. The outer life matures, but the real issue is that we are children internally and demonstrate it with immaturity.

David was king and still acting like a child on the inside. He was acting like a child to what he wanted and what he knew was not his. We all know about his situation with Uriah's wife. He was mature, but his actions were childish and selfish.

David becomes a modern-day metaphor for us to demonstrate that we are still children in many ways. We are grown on the outside but a kid on the inside. We look at our lives as children. Are we, as apostles and prophets ignoring our childish ways? And we are still trying to lead others.

What is the answer? Look again at *1 Corinthians 13:11* and see a keyword, and that is "but." You can put away your childish ways, but that will not make you a man or a woman. Again David was a full-grown man and still was a child on the inside.

Throughout the Body of Christ, we have apostles and prophets who are fully grown and yet still demonstrate childish behavior. They are of age and in positions of authority, yet their influence is that of a child. They have not put away their childish ways.

There is no understanding of what it means. That is a choice they have not exercised because they lack understanding of the power of changing a mentality.

Can you understand that many of us in the apostolic and prophetic are still childish? We have outgrown how we communicate, think and act; we have only done this on the outside, not on the inside. This is where we need to be to make the changes.

How many of us will admit that we have outgrown how we sometimes act, speak one thing, and actually mean something different? Do we realize that we need to put some things away? What are we loyal to?

We are to put some things away, like our childish actions. They are systematically killing us and destroying our relationships with each other. Our growth as foundation pieces of the gospel will never be realized until we understand that it works both ways.

Our ability to respond as a child diminishes when we take charge and put some things out of our life. Our childish ways restrict us from operating in the glory of God. Look at apostle Paul and how he moved from his selfish ways and quickly matured into a leader of inspiration and revelation.

The Apostle Paul is direct when he says to put them away. He is talking about our ways. Let go of the childish ways that restrict us from reaching our destiny. Look at Paul's life, and you will see that he put his childish ways away. Look at everything he let go of in his life.

Paul teaches us that we must identify what is childish in our lives. Unless we identify it every time, we will carry weight and issues that have nothing to do with our progress. I am saying that we must put away what we have been defending with our actions for so long.

What do we need to accomplish as an apostle or a prophet? The power of life and death is in the tongue; if you are unwilling to change, you will not grow.

Understanding will heal a multitude of issues. We refer to understanding as the truth that we stand on and under. The power of understanding is what will separate us from being a child to being an adult. This is how and why we must move forward from where we are at and not skip today for tomorrow.

The mentality of a mature prophet or a mature apostle is all about understanding. What we choose to understand or not understand is killing us as apostles or prophets.

When the apostles and prophets of this generation learn how to pull themselves from where they started, then and only then will we make a difference in the lives of God's people through our actions. This is the process of visualization and seeing in our personal Cave of Adullam.

Final Thought:

Living in an ever-changing world, it is good to know that God is still God. The ability to grow in the prophetic is reflected in our daily lives: what we do and how we do reflections in our day-by-day routine.

Study yourself, and you will find a new you. Become a friend to yourself. You have to opportunity to be the best version of yourself. The key to growing and moving forth is what God has put within you. I love David. He is not perfect and has his faults, but he is cool under stress, and his struggle to become king is as much an inner work as it is an outer work in his life.

David is the prototype prophet God will send into multiple cultures and use mighty. He has already proved it as we study and look closely at his life. We all are candidates for visualization as we all have a cave we must go to see. Thank you for reading Visualization; The Prophet Sees In Adullam.

Apostle Ken Cox

About The Author

Apostle Ken Cox started serving God in 1994 after a series of unforeseen life failures. Out of the military and seemly starting life over again, by 2000, Apostle Cox had found his life calling as a Prophet. The challenge of learning and understanding presented a new frontier. Apostle Cox dove into the process and has now emerged as a well-traveled prophet who serves the Body of Christ as an Apostle.

Apostle Cox, along with his wife, Prophetess Sabina Cox are the leaders of Where Eagles Fly Fellowship Inc., a fellowship of prophets and apostle across the USA and beyond who are dedicated and focused on establishing the prophetic gift back into society as they raise up prophets around the country and abroad.

Apostle Cox and Prophetess Cox are available for Revivals, Conferences and Meetings. They have been featured in meetings and sought-after to teach and instruct the prophetic for ministries seeking to learn more about the gift. Apostle and Prophetess Cox have 3 children and 4 grandkids as of this writing and currently reside in Durham, NC. Contact them through the Where Eagles Fly office at 919-695-3375 or 919-213-1328 or at www.whereeaglesfly.us.

Index

I

J

www.ingramcontent.com/pod-product-compliance
Lightning Source LLC
Chambersburg PA
CBHW071407120626
46546CB00002B/850